NATEF Correlated Task Sheets

for

Automotive Engines

Theory and Servicing

Ninth Edition

James D. Halderman

 Pearson

330 Hudson Street, NY NY 10013

Vice President, Portfolio Management: Andrew Gilfillan
Portfolio Manager: Tony Webster
Editorial Assistant: Lara Dimmick
Senior Vice President, Marketing: David Gesell
Field Marketing Manager: Thomas Hayward
Marketing Coordinator: Elizabeth MacKenzie-Lamb
Director, Digital Studio and Content Production: Brian Hyland
Managing Producer: Cynthia Zonneveld
Managing Producer: Jennifer Sargunar
Content Producer: Faraz Sharique Ali

Content Producer: Nikhil Rakshit
Manager, Rights Management: Johanna Burke
Operations Specialist: Deidra Smith
Cover Design: Cenveo Publisher Services
Full-Service Project Management and Composition: Kritika Kaushik, Cenveo Publisher Services
Printer/Binder: LSC Communications Menasha
Cover Printer: Phoenix Color
Text Font: Helvetica Neue LT W1G
Copyright ©2018, 2015, 2011

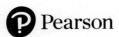

1 16
ISBN-10:   0-13-465403-X
ISBN-13: 978-0-13-465403-4

Table of Contents

v

Shop Safety Checklist

Meets NATEF Task: Not specified by NATEF

Name _____ Date _____ Time on Task _____

Make/Model/Year _____ VIN _____ Evaluation: 4 3 2 1

_____ 1. Walk through the shop(s) area of the school or a local shop or dealership and check for the following items:

      a. Shields on bench or pedestal grinders   Yes___ No___ NA___

      b. Exhaust hoses in good repair   Yes___ No___ NA___

      c. Fire extinguisher installed and charged   Yes___ No___ NA___

      d. First aid kit visible and fully stocked   Yes___ No___ NA___

      e. Fire blanket visible and useable   Yes___ No___ NA___

      f. Eye wash station visible and usable   Yes___ No___ NA___

_____ 2. List anything that should be included in a safe shop that was not present.

      _____

      _____

      _____

      _____

_____ 3. What items of personal protective equipment were being worn by service technicians?

      a. Safety glasses/face shield   Yes___ No___ NA___

      b. Protective gloves   Yes___ No___ NA___

      c. Hearing protection   Yes___ No___ NA___

      d. Bump cap   Yes___ No___ NA___

Fire Extinguisher

Meets NATEF Task: Not specified by NATEF

Name _____ Date _____ Time on Task _____

Make/Model/Year _____ VIN _____ Evaluation: 4   3   2   1

_____ **1.** Describe the location of the fire extinguishers in your building or shop and note the

last inspection dates.

Type of Extinguisher	Location	Inspection Date
_____	_____	_____
_____	_____	_____
_____	_____	_____
_____	_____	_____

_____ **2.** Do any of the fire extinguishers need to be charged?

_____ Yes (which ones) _____

_____ No

_____ **3.** Where can the fire extinguishers be recharged? List the name and telephone number

of the company. _____ _____

_____ **4.** What is the cost to recharge the fire extinguishers?

a. Water =   _____

b. CO_2 =   _____

c. Dry chemical =   _____

Safety Data Sheet (SDS)

Meets NATEF Task: Not specified by NATEF

Name _____ **Date** _____ **Time on Task** _____

Make/Model/Year _____ **VIN** _____ **Evaluation: 4   3   2   1**

_____ **1.** Locate the SDS sheets and describe their location_____

_____

_____ **2.** Select three commonly used chemicals or solvents. Record the following information
from the SDS:

• **Product name** _____

        chemical name(s) _____

        Does the chemical contain "chlor" or "fluor" which may indicate hazardous

        materials? **Yes** _____   **No** _____

        flash point = _____ (hopefully above 140° F)

        pH _____ (7 = neutral, higher than 7 = caustic (base), lower than 7 = acid)

• **Product name** _____

        chemical name(s) _____

        Does the chemical contain "chlor" or "fluor" which may indicate hazardous

        materials? **Yes** _____   **No** _____

        flash point = _____ (hopefully above 140° F)

        pH _____ (7 = neutral, higher than 7 = caustic (base), lower than 7 = acid)

• **Product name** _____

        chemical name(s) _____

        Does the chemical contain "chlor" or "fluor" which may indicate hazardous

        materials? **Yes** _____   **No** _____

        flash point = _____ (hopefully above 140° F)

      pH _____ **(7 = neutral, higher than 7 = caustic (base), lower than 7 = acid)**

Thread Repair

Meets NATEF Task: (A1-A-14) Perform fastener and thread repair (P-1)

Name _____ Date _____ Time on Task _____

Make/Model/Year _____ VIN _____ Evaluation: 4 3 2 1

_____ **1.** Drill a hole in a piece of metal about ¼ inch thick and then thread it using a tap.

Install a bolt into the thread hole and either break it off or cut the bolt flush with the

surface.

Instructor OK _____

_____ **2.** Remove the broken off bolt using an easy out or other tool.

Instructor OK _____

_____ **3.** Using an old engine block, drill out one threaded hole in the block and install a

threaded insert, following the instructions that came with the thread insert kit.

Instructor OK _____

We Support
NATEF

Hand Tool Identification

Meets NATEF Task: Not specified by NATEF

Name _____ Date _____ Time on Task _____

Make/Model/Year _____ VIN _____ Evaluation: 4 3 2 1

_____ 1. List the sizes of **wrenches** you have in
your tool box. _____

_____

_____

What sizes are missing or will need to be

purchased? _____

_____

_____ 2. List the sizes of the **1/4 inch drive sockets** you have in your tool box. _____

_____

What sizes are missing or will need to be purchased? _____

_____

_____ 3. List the sizes of the **3/8 inch drive sockets** you have in your tool box. _____

_____

What sizes are missing or will need to be purchased? _____

_____

_____ 4. List the sizes of the **1/2 inch drive sockets** you have in your tool box. _____

_____

What sizes are missing or will need to be purchased? _____

_____

_____ 5. List the **other tools** you have in your tool box including hammers, screwdrivers,

pliers, and other items. _____

_____

List additional tools that you wish to add to your tool box. _____

_____

6

Power and Shop Equipment Safety Survey

Meets NATEF Task: Not specified by NATEF

Name _____ **Date** _____ **Time on Task** _____

Make/Model/Year _____ **VIN** _____ **Evaluation: 4 3 2 1**

_____ 1. Check the power and shop equipment in the shop, at a local shop, or dealer. Where was this survey taken? _____

_____ 2. List all shop equipment, such as hoists, floor jacks, and cranes, and not whether they are equipped with all needed safety devices.

Shop Equipment	**Safety devices? If not, list:**
_____	Yes__ No__ (describe) _____
_____	Yes__ No__ (describe) _____
_____	Yes__ No__ (describe) _____
_____	Yes__ No__ (describe) _____
_____	Yes__ No__ (describe) _____
_____	Yes__ No__ (describe) _____

_____ 3. List all power equipment, such as trouble lights, grinders, etc. and note whether they are equipped with all needed safety devices.

Power Equipment	**Safety devices? If not, list:**
_____	Yes__ No__ (describe) _____
_____	Yes__ No__ (describe) _____
_____	Yes__ No__ (describe) _____
_____	Yes__ No__ (describe) _____
_____	Yes__ No__ (describe) _____

7

Oxy-Acetylene Torch Usage

Meets NATEF Task: Not specified by NATEF

Name _____ Date _____ Time on Task _____

Make/Model/Year _____ VIN _____ Evaluation: 4 3 2 1

Caution: Proper operation of an oxy-acetylene torch requires proper instruction and willingness to follow all safety precautions.

Instructor check that proper instruction has been given on the safe use of the oxy-acetylene torch.

_____

_____ **1.** Setup the torch and pressures to heat metal.

Oxygen pressure set to _____

Acetylene pressure set to _____

Instructor's OK _____

_____ **2.** Setup torch to cut metal.

Oxygen pressure set to _____

Acetylene pressure set to _____

Instructor's OK _____

8

Vehicle Hoisting

Meets NATEF Task: Not specified by NATEF

Name _____ Date _____ Time on Task _____

Make/Model/Year _____ VIN _____ Evaluation: 4 3 2 1

Getting Ready to Hoist the Vehicle

_____ **1.** Drive the vehicle into position to be hoisted (lifted) being certain to center the vehicle in the stall.

_____ **2.** Pull the vehicle forward until the front tire rests on the tire pad (if equipped).

_____ **3.** Place the gear selector into the park position (if the vehicle has an automatic transmission/transaxle) or in neutral (if the vehicle has a manual transmission/transaxle) and firmly apply the parking brake.

_____ **4.** Lower the driver's side window before exiting the vehicle. (This step helps prevent keys from being accidentally being locked in the vehicle.)

_____ **5.** Position the arms and hoist pads under the frame or pinch-weld seams of the body.

Hoisting the Vehicle

_____ **6.** Slowly raise the vehicle about one foot (30 cm) off the ground and check the stability of the vehicle by attempting to move the vehicle on the lift.

_____ **7.** If the vehicle is stable and all pads are properly positioned under the vehicle, continue hoisting the vehicle to the height needed.

NOTE: Best working conditions are at chest or elbow level.

_____ **8.** Be sure the safety latches have engaged before working under the vehicle.

Lowering the Vehicle

_____ **9.** To lower the vehicle, raise the hoist slightly, then release the safety latches.

_____ **10.** Lower the vehicle using the proper operating and safety release levers.

CAUTION: Do not look away while lowering the vehicle. One side of the vehicle could become stuck or something (or someone) could get under the vehicle.

_____ **11.** After lowering the hoist arms all the way to the floor, move the arms so that they will not be hit when the vehicle is driven out of the stall.

9

Micrometer

Meets NATEF Task: Not specified by NATEF

Name _____ **Date** _____ **Time on Task** _____

Make/Model/Year _____ **VIN** _____ **Evaluation:** 4 3 2 1

A micrometer is the most used measuring instrument in engine service and repair. The thimble rotates over the barrel on a screw that has 40 threads per inch. Every revolution of the thimble moves the spindle 0.025 inch. The thimble is graduated into 25 equally spaced lines; therefore, each line represents 0.001 inch. Measure and record the following engine components.

_____ **1.** Pushrod diameter = _____

_____ **2.** Intake valve stem diameter = _____

_____ **3.** Exhaust valve stem diameter = _____

_____ **4.** Camshaft bearing diameter = _____

_____ **5.** Piston diameter = _____

Check the factory specifications for exact location on the piston to measure the diameter.

Location = _____

_____ **6.** Crankshaft main bearing journal diameter = _____

_____ **7.** Crankshaft rod bearing journal diameter = _____

Vernier Dial Caliper

Meets NATEF Task: Not specified by NATEF

Name _____ Date _____ Time on Task _____

Make/Model/Year _____ VIN _____ Evaluation: 4 3 2 1

A Vernier dial caliper is usually used to measure the outside diameter or length of a component such as a piston diameter or crankshaft and camshaft bearing journal diameter. Use a venire dial caliper to measure the following items.

_____ 1. Pushrod diameter = _____

_____ 2. Intake valve stem diameter = _____

_____ 3. Exhaust valve stem diameter = _____

_____ 4. Camshaft bearing diameter = _____

_____ 5. Piston diameter = _____

      Check the factory specifications for exact location on the piston to measure the diameter.

      Location = _____

_____ 6. Crankshaft main bearing journal diameter = _____

_____ 7. Crankshaft rod bearing journal diameter = _____

Feeler Gauge

Meets NATEF Task: Not specified by NATEF

Name _____ **Date** _____ **Time on Task** _____

Make/Model/Year _____ **VIN** _____ **Evaluation:** 4 3 2 1

A feeler gauge (also known as a thickness gauge) is an accurately manufactured strip of metal that is used to determine the gap or clearance between two components. Use a feeler gauge to check the following.

_____ **1.** Piston ring end gap = _____

   Specification = _____ (normally 0.004 in. per inch of bore)

   OK _____ **NOT OK** _____

_____ **2.** Piston ring side clearance = _____

   Specification = _____ (normally 0.001 to 0.003 in.)

   OK _____ **NOT OK** _____

_____ **3.** Piston-to-cylinder wall clearance = _____

   Specification = _____ (normally 0.001 to 0.003 in.)

   OK _____ **NOT OK** _____

_____ **4.** Connecting rod side clearance = _____

   Specification = _____

   OK _____ **NOT OK** _____

Straight-Edge

Meets NATEF Task: Not specified by NATEF

Name _____ Date _____ Time on Task _____

Make/Model/Year _____ VIN _____ Evaluation: 4   3   2   1

A straight edge is a precision ground metal measuring gauge that is used to check the flatness of engine components when used with a feeler gauge. Use a straight edge to check the flatness of the following.

_____ **1.** Cylinder heads _____

Specification = _____

OK _____   **NOT OK** _____

_____ **2.** Cylinder block deck _____

Specification = _____

OK _____   **NOT OK** _____

_____ **3.** Straightness of the main bearing bores (saddles) _____

Specification = _____

OK _____   **NOT OK** _____

Dial Indicator

Meets NATEF Task: Not specified by NATEF

Name _____ Date _____ Time on Task _____

Make/Model/Year _____ VIN _____ Evaluation: 4 3 2 1

A dial indicator is a precision measuring instrument used to measure clearance to within thousandths of an inch. Use a dial indicator to measure the following.

_____ **1.** Crankshaft end play = _____

        Specification = _____

        OK _____   **NOT OK** _____

_____ **2.** Crankshaft runout = _____

        Specification = _____

        OK _____   **NOT OK** _____

_____ **3.** Valve guide = _____

        Specification = _____

        OK _____   **NOT OK** _____

_____ **4.** Camshaft runout = _____

        Specification = _____

        OK _____   **NOT OK** _____

Telescopic Gauge

Meets NATEF Task: Not specified by NATEF

Name _____ Date _____ Time on Task _____

Make/Model/Year _____ VIN _____ Evaluation: 4 3 2 1

A telescopic gauge is used with a micrometer to measure the inside diameter of a hole or bore. The inside diameter of a hole can be measured by inserting a telescopic gauge into the bore and rotating the handle lock to allow the arms of the gauge to contact the inside bore of the cylinder. Tighten the handle lock and remove the gauge from the cylinder. Use a micrometer to measure the telescopic gauge. Use a telescopic gauge with a micrometer and measure the following.

_____ **1.** Camshaft bearing bore = _____

   Specification = _____

   OK _____   **NOT OK** _____

_____ **2.** Main bearing bore (housing bore) measurement = _____

   Specification = _____

   OK _____   **NOT OK** _____

_____ **3.** Cylinder bore = _____

   Specification = _____

   OK _____   **NOT OK** _____

_____ **4.** Connecting rod big-end bore

   measurement = _____

   Specification = _____

   OK _____   **NOT OK** _____

_____ **5.** Connecting rod small-end bore measurement = _____

   Specification = _____

   OK _____   **NOT OK** _____

Work Order

Meets NATEF Task: (A1-A-1) Complete work order and complete necessary customer and vehicle information. (P-1)

Name _____ Date _____ Time on Task _____

Make/Model/Year _____ VIN _____ Evaluation: 4 3 2 1

_____ 1. List the items about the **vehicle** that should be included on the work order (also called a repair order - R.O).

      a. _____   e. _____

      b. _____   f. _____

      c. _____   g. _____

      d. _____   h. _____

_____ 2. List the information about the **driver/owner** that should be included on the work order.

      a. _____

      b. _____

      c. _____

      d. _____

_____ 3. List the three Cs (concern, cause, and correction) that the service technician should write on the work order for a repair that includes a diagnosis of the problem (concern), the replacement of a part, and the verification of the repair.

      a. _____

      b. _____

      c. _____

Service Manual Usage

Meets NATEF Task: (A1-A-2) Research Vehicle and Service Information, Vehicle History and TSBs (P-1)

Name _____ **Date** _____ **Time on Task** _____

Make/Model/Year _____ **VIN** _____ **Evaluation:** 4 3 2 1

Look up the following service information and record the page number or document number where the information was found.

Spark plug number: _____ location found _____

Spark plug gap: _____ location found _____

Number of quarts of oil for an oil change: _____ location found _____

Viscosity of engine oil recommended: _____ location found _____

Air filter part number: _____ location found _____

Fuel filter part number: _____ location found _____

AC generator (alternator) output: _____ amps location found _____

Bore and stroke of the engine: bore _____ stroke _____ location found _____

Valve cover bolt torque specification: _____ location found _____

17

Vehicle Safety Certification Label

Meets NATEF Task: (A1-A-3) Locate and interpret vehicle and major component
identification numbers (P-1)

Name _____ Date _____ Time on Task _____

Make/Model/Year _____ VIN _____ Evaluation: 4 3 2 1

_____ **1.** Describe the location of the Vehicle Safety Certification Label (usually located on the driver's side pillar post).

_____

GM	MFD BY GENERAL MOTORS OF CANADA LTD.		
	DATE	GVWR	GAWR FRT	GAWR RR
	06/02	2071 KG	1115 KG	956 KG
		4565 LB	2458 LB	2107 LB

THIS VEHICLE CONFORMS TO ALL APPLICABLE U.S. FEDERAL MOTOR VEHICLE SAFETY, BUMPER, AND THEFT PREVENTION STANDARDS IN EFFECT ON THE DATE OF MANUFACTURE SHOWN ABOVE.

2G1WF52E839104270   TYPE: PASS CAR

_____ **2.** What is the month and year the vehicle was manufactured?

Month = _____

Year = _____

_____ **3.** What is the gross vehicle weight rating (GVWR)?

_____

_____ **4.** What is the gross axle weight rating (GAWR)?

_____

_____ **5.** Is the exact date of manufacture listed on the label?

____ Yes   Month = _____   Day = _____   Year = _____

____ No

18

VIN Code

Meets NATEF Task: (A1-A-4) Locate and interpret vehicle identification numbers. (P-1)

Name _____ Date _____ Time on Task _____

Make/Model/Year _____ VIN _____ Evaluation: 4 3 2 1

- The first number or letter designates the **country of origin** = _____

1 = United States	6 = Australia	L = China	V = France
2 = Canada	8 = Argentina	R = Taiwan	W = Germany
3 = Mexico	9 = Brazil	S = England	X = Russia
4 = United States	J = Japan	T = Czechoslovakia	Y = Sweden
5 = United States	K = Korea	U = Romania	Z = Italy

- The model of the vehicle is commonly the fourth or fifth character. **Model?** _____
- The eighth character is often the engine code. (Some engines cannot be determined by the VIN number.) **Engine code:** _____
- The tenth character represents the year on all vehicles. See the following chart.

VIN Year Chart (The pattern repeats every 30 years.)   Year? _____

A = 1980/2010	J = 1988/2018	T = 1996/2026	4 = 2004/2034
B = 1981/2011	K = 1989/2019	V = 1997/2027	5 = 2005/2035
C = 1982/2012	L = 1990/2020	W = 1998/2028	6 = 2006/2036
D = 1983/2013	M = 1991/2021	X = 1999/2029	7 = 2007/2037
E = 1984/2014	N = 1992/2022	Y = 2000/2030	8 = 2008/2038
F = 1985/2015	P = 1993/2023	1 = 2001/2031	9 = 2009/2039
G = 1986/2016	R = 1994/2024	2 = 2002/2032	
H = 1987/2017	S = 1995/2025	3 = 2003/2033	

19

Vehicle Service History

Meets NATEF Task: (A6-A-3) Research vehicle service information, vehicle service history and TSBs. (P-1)

Name _____ Date _____ Time on Task _____

Make/Model/Year _____ VIN _____ Evaluation: 4 3 2 1

_____ **1.** Search vehicle history (check all that apply).

       ____ Computerized data base (electronic file if previous service work)

       ____ Files (hard copy of previous service work)

       ____ Customer information (verbal)

       ____ Other (describe) _____

_____ **2.** What electrical-related repairs have been performed in this vehicle? _____

_____

_____

_____

_____ **3.** From the information obtained, has the vehicle been serviced regularly?

       ____ Yes (describe the service intervals) _____

_____

_____

       ____ No (why?) _____

_____

_____ **4.** Based on the service history information, is the service record helpful? Why or why not? _____

_____

_____

20

Technical Service Bulletins

Meets NATEF Task: (A6-A-3) Research vehicle service information, vehicle service history and TSBs. (P-1)

Name _____ Date _____ Time on Task _____

Make/Model/Year _____ VIN _____ Evaluation: 4 3 2 1

_____ **1.** Technical service bulletins can be accessed through (check all that apply):

_____ Internet site(s), specify _____

_____ Paper bulletins, specify source _____

_____ CD ROM bulletins, specify source _____

_____ Other (describe) _____

_____ **2.** List all electrical-related technical service bulletins that pertain to the vehicle/engine being serviced.

Number	**Description/Correction**
_____	_____
_____	_____
_____	_____
_____	_____

_____ **3.** Based on this research, is the information located helpful?

_____ Yes, why? _____

_____ No, why not? _____

21

We Support
NATEF

Vehicle Emission Control Information

Meets NATEF Task: (A1-A-4) Research vehicle and service information (P-1)

Name _____ Date _____ Time on Task _____

Make/Model/Year _____ VIN _____ Evaluation: 4 3 2 1

_____ **1.** Locate the vehicle emission control information (VECI) sticker and describe its

location: _____

TOYOTA	VEHICLE EMISSION CONTROL INFORMATION
	TOYOTA MOTOR CORPORATION

TEST GROUP : 7TYXV01.5HC1
SFI, A/FS, WU-TWC, HO2S, TWC   EVAP. FAMILY : 7TYXR0030A42
                                                                     1.5 LITER

ENGINE TUNE-UP SPECIFICATIONS FOR ALL ALTITUDES

| VALVE CLEARANCE | INTAKE | 0.17-0.23 mm (0.007-0.009 in.) |
| (ENGINE AT COLD) | EXHAUST | 0.27-0.33 mm (0.011-0.013 in.) |

NO OTHER ADJUSTMENTS NEEDED.

THIS VEHICLE CONFORMS TO U. S. EPA REGULATIONS APPLICABLE
TO GASOLINE-FUELED 2007 MODEL YEAR NEW TIER 2 BIN 3
MOTOR VEHICLES AND TO CALIFORNIA REGULATIONS APPLICABLE TO
2007 MODEL YEAR NEW LEV-II SULEV PASSENGER CARS.

CATALYST

OBD II CERTIFIED

8V

21160   1NZ-FXE   USA&CANADA

_____ **2.** List what service information is included on the sticker: _____

_____

_____

_____ **3.** List emission control devices on the vehicle: _____

_____

_____ **4.** What is the U.S. Federal emission rating of the vehicle? _____

_____ **5.** What is the California emission rating of the vehicle? _____

22

Gasoline Engine Identification

Meets NATEF Task: (A1-A-4) Locate and interpret vehicle and major component identification numbers. (P-1)

Name _____ Date _____ Time on Task _____

Make/Model/Year _____ VIN _____ Evaluation: 4 3 2 1

_____ **1.** Number of cylinders = _____ Arrangement of cylinders = _____

_____ **2.** Number and arrangement of camshafts = _____

_____ **3.** Bore = _____ Stroke = _____ Cu. in. = _____ cc = _____ Liters = _____

_____ **4.** Rated HP = _____ @ RPM _____

_____ **5.** Rated torque = _____ @ RPM _____

_____ **6.** Compression ratio = _____

_____ **7.** Recommended octane of gasoline required = _____

_____ **8.** The block is constructed of: _____ cast iron _____ aluminum

_____ **9.** Cylinder head(s) is constructed of: _____ cast iron _____ aluminum

_____ **10.** Intake manifold is: _____ one piece _____ two pieces (upper and lower) and is

constructed of: _____ cast iron _____ aluminum _____ composite

23

General Engine Specification

Meets NATEF Task: (A1-A-4) Locate and interpret vehicle and major component identification numbers. (P-1)

Name _____ Date _____ Time on Task _____

Make/Model/Year _____ VIN _____ Evaluation: 4 3 2 1

_____ **1.** Engine type (V-6, V-8, etc.) = _____

_____ **2.** Bore = _____

_____ **3.** Stroke = _____

_____ **4.** Compression ratio = _____

_____ **5.** Displacement: cubic inches = _____

cc = _____   liter = _____

_____ **6.** Horsepower = _____ @ _____RPM

_____ **7.** Torque = _____ @ _____RPM

_____ **8.** Firing order = _____

_____ **9.** Engine oil capacity = _____

_____ **10.** Cylinder block material = _____

_____ **11.** Crankshaft material (forged steel, cast iron) = _____

_____ **12.** Cylinder head material = _____

_____ **13.** Connecting rod material (forged steel, powdered metal, etc.) = _____

COMPRESSION RATIO = 8:1

CLEARANCE VOLUME

CYLINDER VOLUME

1
2
3
4
5
6
7
8

PISTON DISPLACEMENT

BOTTOM DEAD CENTER

TOP DEAD CENTER

24

Diesel Engine Identification

Meets NATEF Task: (A1-A-4) Locate and interpret vehicle and major component identification numbers (VIN, vehicle certification labels, and calibration decals). (P-1)

Name _____ Date _____ Time on Task _____

Make/Model/Year _____ VIN _____ Evaluation: 4 3 2 1

Check service information and determine the following information.

_____ 1. Compression ratio = _____

_____ 2. Fuel pressure (lift pump) = _____

_____ 3. Fuel pressure (common rail) = _____

_____ 4. Oil viscosity required = _____

_____ 5. Bore = _____

_____ 6. Stroke = _____

_____ 7. Cubic inch displacement = _____

_____ 8. Cubic centimeter displacement = _____

_____ 9. Liter displacement = _____

_____ 10. Fuel filter replacement interval = _____
_____

_____ 11. Air filter replacement interval = _____

_____ 12. Oil change interval = _____

_____ 13. Horsepower @ RPM = _____ @ _____RPM

_____ 14. Torque @ RPM = _____ @ _____ RPM

_____ 15. Maximum engine speed _____

25

Diesel Engine Emission Control Systems

Meets NATEF Task: (A1-A-4) Locate and interpret vehicle and major component identification numbers (VIN, vehicle certification labels, and calibration decals). (P-1)

Name _____ **Date** _____ **Time on Task** _____

Make/Model/Year _____ **VIN** _____ **Evaluation:** 4 3 2 1

_____ 1. Check the vehicle emission control information (VECI) underhood sticker and

determine which of the following emission control devices are used. (Check all that

apply.)

                _____ EGR

                _____ PCV

                _____ DPE

                _____ Other (describe) _____

_____ 2. Is the engine equipped with an electronic throttle control (ETC) system?

         Yes _____ No _____

_____ 3. Is the engine equipped with a throttle plate to help control EGR?

         Yes _____ No _____ If yes, describe the location: _____

_____ 4. Are the EGR gases cooled before they enter the engine?

         Yes _____ No _____ If yes, describe the method of cooling and the location:

_____

26

Flexible Fuel Vehicle Identification

Meets NATEF Task: (A8-A-3)

Research applicable vehicle and service information. (P-1)

Name _____ Date _____ Time on Task _____

Make/Model/Year _____ VIN _____ Evaluation: 4 3 2 1

Many vehicles are manufactured that are capable of operating on fuels other than, or in addition to, regular gasoline. Check service information and determine where it is stated on the vehicle if it is capable of using a fuel other than gasoline and what fuel(s) it is capable of using. Select one vehicle model from each major manufacturer.

Manufacturer	Model	Year	Location of Information	Fuel(s)
General Motors				
DaimlerChrysler				
Honda				
Toyota				
Nissan				
Hyundai				
Kia				
Other				
Other				

27

Alternative Fuel Power and Economy Specifications

Meets NATEF Task: (A8-A-3)

Research applicable vehicle and service information. (P-1)

Name _____ Date _____ Time on Task _____

Make/Model/Year _____ VIN _____ Evaluation: 4 3 2 1

With vehicles that are designed to use gasoline and alternative fuel, such as E-85, manufacturers usually rate the horsepower, torque, and EPA fuel economy ratings separately. Select four flex-fuel vehicles and using service information locate the values for both gasoline and the alternative fuel.

Vehicle #1 Make _____ Model _____ Year _____ Engine _____

	HP	Torque	City MPG	Highway MPG
Gasoline				
Alternative Fuel				

Vehicle #2 Make _____ Model _____ Year _____ Engine _____

	HP	Torque	City MPG	Highway MPG
Gasoline				
Alternative Fuel				

Vehicle #3 Make _____ Model _____ Year _____ Engine _____

	HP	Torque	City MPG	Highway MPG
Gasoline				
Alternative Fuel				

Vehicle #4 Make _____ Model _____ Year _____ Engine _____

	HP	Torque	City MPG	Highway MPG
Gasoline				
Alternative Fuel				

28

We Support

Gasoline Engine Identification

Meets NATEF Task: (A8-A-4) Locate and interpret vehicle and major component identification information. (P-1)

Name _____ **Date** _____ **Time on Task** _____

Make/Model/Year _____ **VIN** _____ **Evaluation:** 4 3 2 1

_____ **1.** Number of cylinders = _____   Arrangement of cylinders = _____

_____ **2.** Number and arrangement of camshafts = _____

_____ **3.** Bore = _____ Stroke = _____ Cu. in. = _____ cc = _____ Liters = _____

_____ **4.** Rated HP = _____ @ RPM _____

_____ **5.** Rated torque = _____ @ RPM _____

_____ **6.** Compression ratio = _____

_____ **7.** Recommended octane of gasoline required = _____

_____ **8.** The block is constructed of: _____ cast iron _____ aluminum

_____ **9.** Cylinder head(s) is constructed of: _____ cast iron _____ aluminum

_____ **10.** Intake manifold is: _____ one piece _____ two pieces (upper and lower) and is

constructed of: _____ cast iron _____ aluminum _____ composite

_____ **11.** Casting numbers on the block _____ Cylinder head(s) _____

Crankshaft _____

Alcohol Content in Gasoline

Meets NATEF Task: (A8-D-2) Check fuel for contaminants and quality; determine necessary action. (P-3)

Name _____ Date _____ Time on Task _____

Make/Model/Year _____ VIN _____ Evaluation: 4 3 2 1

Take the following steps when testing gasoline for alcohol content.

_____ 1. Pour suspect gasoline into a small clean beaker or glass container.

DO NOT SMOKE OR RUN THE TEST AROUND SOURCES OF IGNITION!

_____ 2. Carefully fill the graduated cylinder to the 10-mL mark.

_____ 3. Add 2 mL of water to the graduated cylinder by counting the number of drops from an eyedropper. (Before performing the test, the eyedropper must be calibrated to determine how many drops equal 2.0 mL.)

_____ 4. Put the stopper in the cylinder and shake vigorously for 1 minute. Relieve built-up pressure by occasionally removing the stopper. Alcohol dissolves in water and will drop to the bottom of the cylinder.

_____ 5. Place the cylinder on a flat surface and let it stand for 2 minutes.

_____ 6. Take a reading near the bottom of the cylinder at the boundary between the two liquids.

_____ 7. For percent of alcohol in gasoline, subtract 2 from the reading and multiply by 10.

For example,   The reading is 3.1 mL: 3.1 - 2 = 1.1 X 10 = 11% alcohol

The reading is 2.0 mL: 2 - 2 = 0 X 10 = 0% alcohol (no alcohol)

If the increase in volume is 0.2% or less, it may be assumed that the test gasoline contains no alcohol. Alcohol content can also be checked using an electronic tester.

_____ 8. Based on the test results, what action is

necessary? _____

_____

_____

_____

30

Test and Replace Coolant

Meets NATEF Task: (A1-D-7) Test coolant; drain and recover coolant; flush and refill cooling system with recommended coolant; bleed air as required. (P-1)

Name _____ Date _____ Time on Task _____

Make/Model/Year _____ VIN _____ Evaluation: 4 3 2 1

_____ **1.** Check service information for the recommended coolant testing, recover, flushing, and refilling procedures.

_____

_____

_____

_____ **2.** What is the recommended coolant? _____

_____ **3.** Is the cooling system equipped with bleeder valves to help with bleeding trapped air from the cooling system when it is refilled?

_____ **No** _____ **Yes** (describe location) _____

_____

31

Cooling System Tests

Meets NATEF Task: (A1-A-2) Identify and interpret engine concern; determine necessary action. (P-1)

Name _____ Date _____ Time on Task _____

Make/Model/Year _____ VIN _____ Evaluation: 4 3 2 1

_____ 1. Check service information for the specified cooling system tests and specifications.

_____

_____ 2. Pressure test the cooling system using a hand-operated pressure tester as per the tester manufacturer's instructions. Results:

    _____ OK – pressure held
    _____ NOT OK – pressure dropped
    Describe the fault found: _____

_____ 3. Pressure test the pressure cap using a hand-operated pressure tester.

    _____ OK – pressure held
    _____ NOT OK

_____ 4. Check the cooling system for presence of combustion gases. Check the procedure used.

    _____ Exhaust gas analyzer checking for HC emissions
    _____ Coated paper that changes color
    _____ Liquid tester that changes color
    _____ Other (describe) _____

_____ 5. Results of combustion gas test:

    _____ Negative (no combustion gases discovered in coolant)
    _____ Positive (combustion gas discovered in coolant)

_____ 6. Check temperature of cooling system using an infrared pyrometer or other suitable temperature measuring instrument.

    _____ Check the radiator for cool areas, which could indicate blockages
    _____ Compare temperature of the cooling system hoses to thermostat rating

_____ 7. Based on the cooling system tests, what is the necessary action? _____

32

Engine Cooling System Identification

Meets NATEF Task: (A1-A-3) Research applicable vehicle and service information, vehicle service history, service precautions, and technical service bulletins. (P-1)

Name _____ Date _____ Time on Task _____

Make/Model/Year _____ VIN _____ Evaluation: 4 3 2 1

_____ **1.** Locate the engine coolant temperature sensor (ECT) and describe its location:

_____

_____ **2.** Locate the engine cooling system bleeder valve(s), if equipped, and describe its location:

_____

_____ **3.** The recommended coolant for this engine is:

_____ ethylene glycol (green color)

_____ Dex-Cool™ (orange color)

_____ OAT (organic acid technology) (orange color)

_____ HOAT (hydrid organic acid technology) (green, yellow, blue or orange)

_____ other (specify) _____

_____ **4.** The engine uses:

_____ conventional coolant flow (from the radiator to the block, to the head(s), and then back to the radiator)

_____ reverse flow (from the radiator to the cylinder head(s), to the block, and then back to the radiator)

_____ other (specify) _____

_____ **5.** The thermostat rating is _____ degrees F (_____ degrees C)

_____ **6.** The thermostat is located:

_____ at the inlet side of water pump _____ at the outlet side of water pump

33

Engine Cooling System Inspection

Meets NATEF Task: (A1-D-3) Perform cooling system pressure tests; check coolant condition; inspect and test radiator, pressure cap, coolant recovery tank, and hoses. (P-1)

Name _____ Date _____ Time on Task _____

Make/Model/Year _____ VIN _____ Evaluation: 4   3   2   1

_____ **1.** Inspect the radiator for exterior leaks or clogged
areas due to bugs, dirt, or debris, and clean as required.

OK _____   NOT OK _____

_____ **2.** Pressure test the cooling system. The entire system should hold about 15 psi for 5 minutes, unless there is a leak.

OK _____   NOT OK _____

Location of leak _____

_____ **3.** Pressure test the radiator cap. The cap holds _____ psi.

OK _____   NOT OK _____

_____ **4.** Check the freezing point of the coolant using an hydrometer = _____
[should be -34° F (-37° C) or lower].

OK _____   NOT OK _____

_____ **5.** Check the boiling point of the coolant using an hydrometer = _____.

OK _____   NOT OK _____

TOP TANK

RADIATOR CAP

TUBES

COOLANT FLOW

BOTTOM TANK

TRANSMISSION OIL COOLER

34

Radiator Testing with an Infrared Pyrometer

Meets NATEF Task: (A1-D-3) Perform cooling system pressure tests; check coolant condition; inspect and test radiator, pressure cap, coolant recovery tank, and hoses. (P-1)

Name _____ Date _____ Time on Task _____

Make/Model/Year _____ VIN _____ Evaluation: 4 3 2 1

_____ 1. Check to see if an infrared pyrometer can be aimed to most areas of the radiator from the engine side.

> **NOTE:** The fan(s) shroud may have to be removed to gain access.

_____ 2. What had to be removed to allow access? _____
_____

_____ 3. Start the engine and operate until normal operating temperature is achieved and the thermostat is fully open.

_____ 4. Using an infrared pyrometer, measure the radiator at the inlet, middle, and outlet sections and record the readings.

Inlet = _____ (should be the hottest)
Middle = _____ (should be cooler than the inlet section)
Outlet = _____ (should be cooler than the middle)

OK _____   NOT OK _____

_____ 5. Aim the infrared pyrometer to all sections of the radiator and look for any areas that are cooler than the surroundings which indicate a restricted or clogged portion of the radiator.

OK _____   NOT OK _____

_____ 6. Reinstall any shrouds removed to gain access to the radiator.

_____ 7. Based on the inspection and temperature tests, what is the necessary action?

_____
_____

Accessory Drive Belt Replacement

Meets NATEF Task: (A1-D-4) Inspect, replace, and adjust drive belts, tensioners and pulleys; check pulley and belt alignment. (P-1)

Name _____ Date _____ Time on Task _____

Make/Model/Year _____ VIN _____ Evaluation: 4 3 2 1

_____ **1.** Check service information for the specified drive belt inspection and replacement procedures.

_____

_____

_____ **2.** Inspect the drive belt(s).

      _____ OK

      _____ NOT OK (describe fault)

      _____

      _____

POWER-STEERING PUMP PULLEY   ALTERNATOR PULLEY

TENSIONER

WATER 1=1 PUMP PULLEY

CRANKSHAFT PULLEY

AIR-CONDITIONING COMPRESSOR PULLEY

_____ **3.** Remove and replace the drive belt(s) according to the vehicle manufacturer's recommended procedures.

      Show the instructor removed drive belt(s)
Instructor OK _____

_____ **4.** Carefully inspect pulleys and tensioner.

      _____ OK

      _____ NOT OK (describe fault) _____

      _____

_____ **5.** Install replacement drive belt and check for proper alignment and tension.

Radiator and Heater Hose Replacement

Meets NATEF Task: (A1-D-5) Inspect and replace engine cooling and heater system hoses.
(P-1)

Name _____ Date _____ Time on Task _____

Make/Model/Year _____ VIN _____ Evaluation: 4 3 2 1

_____ 1. Check service information regarding the specified inspection and replacement procedures for coolant system hoses.

_____

_____

_____ 2. Inspect all cooling system hoses for damage.

Heater hoses:
____ OK ____NOT OK
Describe fault(s): _____
_____
_____

CHAFED OR BURNED

SOFT AND SPONGY

Radiator hose:
____ OK ____NOT OK
Describe fault(s): _____
_____
_____

HARDENED

SWOLLEN OR OIL SOAKED

_____ 3. Following the vehicle manufacturer's recommended procedure, replace the cooling system and heater system hose(s). Describe the procedure specified:

_____

_____

_____ 4. Refill the cooling system.

_____ 5. What is the procedure specified to make certain that all of the trapped air in the cooling system has been purged.

_____

_____

_____ 6. Check for leaks after completion.

37

Thermostat Replacement

Meets NATEF Task: (A1-D-6) Inspect, text, and replace thermostat and gasket/seal. (P-1)

Name _____ Date _____ Time on Task _____

Make/Model/Year _____ VIN _____ Evaluation: 4   3   2   1

_____ 1. Check service information and determine the recommended thermostat testing and replacement procedures.

　　　　　 _____

　　　　　 _____

CAUTION: Do not remove the pressure cap until the engine has cooled. The sudden drop in pressure that occurs when the cap is removed can cause the coolant to boil and cause serious burns from the escaping hot coolant.

_____ 2. Drain the cooling system into a suitable container, down to below the level of the thermostat.

_____ 3. Remove the thermostat housing bolts and housing.

_____ 4. What other components had to be removed to gain access to the thermostat housing?

　　　　　 _____　　_____

　　　　　 _____　　_____

_____ 5. Remove the thermostat and discard the gasket. Clean both gasket-sealing surfaces.

_____ 6. Install the replacement thermostat into the recesses in the housing bore.

_____ 7. Install a new gasket and reinstall the thermostat housing and retaining bolts.

_____ 8. Torque the thermostat housing to factory specification.

　　　　　 Thermostat housing bolt torque specification = _____

_____ 9. Refill the cooling system with new coolant.

CAUTION: Be sure to open the cooling system bleeder valves(s), if equipped, to avoid trapping air.

_____ 10. Install the radiator pressure cap and start the engine. Check for leaks and proper cooling system operation.

38

Radiator Replacement

Meets NATEF Task: (A1-D-9) Remove and replace radiator. (P-2)

Name _____ Date _____ Time on Task _____

Make/Model/Year _____ VIN _____ Evaluation: 4 3 2 1

_____ **1.** Check vehicle service information and determine the specified procedure for removal and reinstallation of the radiator.

_____

_____

_____

_____

_____ **2.** Drain the coolant and dispose or recycle.

> **NOTE:** Many vehicle manufacturers recommend that new coolant be installed whenever servicing the cooling system and that the old coolant not be used.

___ Recycled

___ Disposal (describe how the coolant was properly disposed) _____

_____

_____ **3.** Coolant capacity is _____.

_____ **4.** Radiator is removed from the vehicle.   Instructor OK _____

_____ **5.** Radiator is installed in the vehicle.   Instructor OK _____

_____ **6.** Refill the cooling system and bleed air from the system according to the vehicle manufacturer's recommended procedure.

Instructor OK _____

39

Engine Fan Inspection and Testing

Meets NATEF Task: (A1-D-10) Inspect and text fans(s) (electrical or mechanical), fan clutch, fan shroud, and air dams. (P-1)

Name _____ **Date** _____ **Time on Task** _____

Make/Model/Year _____ **VIN** _____ **Evaluation:** 4 3 2 1

_____ **1.** Identify the type of cooling fans.

      _____ Engine driven

      _____ Electric (If electric, one or two fans? _____)

      _____ Hydraulically operated

_____ **2.** If mechanical, check the fan clutch for fluid (silicone fluid) leakage or other damage.

      OK _____   **NOT OK** _____ Describe the fault: _____

_____ **3.** Check the mechanical fan clutch for proper operation by placing cardboard over the front of the radiator and start the engine. Allow the engine to reach normal operating temperature. As the temperature of the coolant increases above the normal temperature range, the fan noise should increase indicating that the fan clutch has engaged.

      OK _____   **NOT OK** _____

_____ **4.** Inspect the fan shroud for damage or if the shroud is missing.

      OK _____   **NOT OK** _____

_____ **5.** Inspect that the air dam underneath the front of the vehicle is in place and not missing or damaged.

      OK _____   **NOT OK** _____

_____ **6.** From the inspection above, what is the necessary action? _____

_____

40

Identify the Cause of Engine Overheating

Meets NATEF Task: (A1-D-14) Identify causes of engine overheating (P-1)

Name _____ **Date** _____ **Time on Task** _____

Make/Model/Year _____ **VIN** _____ **Evaluation:** 4 3 2 1

_____ **1.** Check service information for the recommended procedure to follow when attempting to locate the cause of an engine overheating. Describe the procedure:

_____

_____

_____ **2.** Check all that are specified:

      _____ Compression test

      _____ Cylinder leakage test

      _____ Scan tool diagnosis

      _____ Radiator and cooling system inspection

      _____ Other (describe) _____

_____

41

Engine Lubrication Specifications

Meets NATEF Task: (A1-A-3) Research applicable vehicle and service information, vehicle service history, service precautions, and TSBs. (P-1)

Name _____ Date _____ Time on Task _____

Make/Model/Year _____ VIN _____ Evaluation: 4 3 2 1

_____ **1.** Oil capacity with oil filter change: _____

_____ **2.** Specified oil viscosity (SAE) rating: _____

_____ **3.** Specified oil quality (API) rating: _____

_____ **4.** Oil filter type and number: _____

_____ **5.** Oil capacity without an oil filter change: _____

_____ **6.** Oil pressure specification: _____

_____ **7.** Oil pump type: _____

_____ **8.** Oil pump location: _____

_____ **9.** Oil pump specifications (list all specified measurements):

_____

_____

_____

_____

42

Engine Oil Change

Meets NATEF Task: (A1-D-13) Perform oil and filter change. (P-1)

Name _____ Date _____ Time on Task _____

Make/Model/Year _____ VIN _____ Evaluation: 4 3 2 1

_____ 1. Check the owner's manual, service manual, or technical literature to determine the correct viscosity rating and quantity of oil needed.
   a. recommended viscosity: SAE _____ or SAE _____
   b. Number of quarts (liters): with the filter _____ without the filter _____
   c. American Petroleum Institute rating (if specified) _____

_____ 2. Filter brand and number: Brand _____ Number _____

_____ 3. Hoist the vehicle safely. Position the oil drain unit under the drain plug and raise to a height about 1 foot under the drain plug.

_____ 4. Select the proper size wrench and remove the drain plug and allow the oil to drain into the drain pan.
   HINT: Apply a light force against the drain plug as you rotate it out of the oil pan. Then pull the drain plug away after unthreading the plug all the way. This helps prevent getting oil all over you and the floor!

_____ 5. After all the oil has been drained, install a new sealing washer (if needed) and install the drain plug.

_____ 6. Move the oil drain unit under the filter and remove the old oil filter.

_____ 7. Use a shop cloth and clean the oil filter gasket contact area on the engine block.

_____ 8. Apply a thin coating of engine oil to the rubber gasket on the new oil filter.

_____ 9. Install the new oil filter and hand tighten about 3/4 turn after the gasket contacts the engine block.

_____ 10. Lower the vehicle. Install the recommended quantity of engine oil using a funnel to prevent spilling oil. Replace the oil filler cap.

_____ 11. Start the engine and allow it to idle. The "oil" light should go out within 15 seconds.

_____ 12. Look under the vehicle and check for leaks at the drain plug and the oil filter.

_____ 13. Check the level of the oil again and add as necessary. **Caution:** Do not overfill!

43

Oil Pump Inspection

Meets NATEF Task: (A1-D-2) Inspect oil pump gears or rotors, housing, pressure relief devices, and pump drive; perform necessary action. (P-2)

Name _____ **Date** _____ **Time on Task** _____

Make/Model/Year _____ **VIN** _____ **Evaluation:** 4 3 2 1

_____ **1.** Check service information for the specified oil pump inspection procedures and wear specifications.

_____

_____

_____ **2.** Check the following visually and take measurements as specified in the service information.

a. Oil pump gears or rotors **OK** ____ **NOT OK** ____

Describe faults: _____

_____

b. Oil pump housing **OK** ____ **NOT OK** ____

Describe faults: _____

_____

c. Pressure relief device **OK** ____ **NOT OK** ____

Describe faults: _____

_____

d. Oil pump drive **OK** ____ **NOT OK** ____

Describe faults: _____

_____

_____ **3.** Based on the inspection, what is the necessary action?

_____

44

Auxiliary Oil Coolers

Meets NATEF Task: (A1-D-11) Inspect Auxiliary Oil Coolers; Determine Necessary Action
(P-3)

Name _____ Date _____ Time on Task _____

Make/Model/Year _____ VIN _____ Evaluation: 4 3 2 1

_____ 1. Check service information for the specified inspection procedure for auxiliary oil coolers.

_____

_____

_____ 2. Check all items checked and inspected.

_____ Cooling hoses to the oil cooler

_____ Oil cooler

_____ O-ring seal/gasket for oil filter

_____ Auxiliary hoses (remote oil filter)

_____ Other (describe) _____

_____ 3. Based on the inspection of the auxiliary oil cooler, what is the necessary action?

_____

_____

_____

45

Oil Temperature and Pressure Switches

Meets NATEF Task: (A1-D-12) Inspect, Test, and Replace Oil Temperature and Pressure Switches and Sensors (P-2)

Name _____ Date _____ Time on Task _____

Make/Model/Year _____ VIN _____ Evaluation: 4 3 2 1

_____ 1. Check service information for the specified testing and replacement procedures for oil temperature and oil pressure switches and sensors.

_____

_____

_____ 2. The vehicle is equipped with the following oil switches and sensors (check all that apply).

_____ Oil temperature sensor (describe location) _____

_____ Oil pressure sensor (describe location) _____

_____ Other (describe) _____

_____ 3. List the steps specified for the replacement of the oil pressure switch, oil temperature switch, or sensors.

_____

46

Starting and Charging Voltmeter Test

Meets NATEF Task: (A6-A-7) Demonstrate the proper use of a (DMM) during diagnosis of electrical circuit problems: source voltage, voltage drop, current flow, and resistance. (P-1)

Name _____ Date _____ Time on Task _____

Make/Model/Year _____ VIN _____ Evaluation: 4 3 2 1

Connect the voltmeter red lead to the positive (+) post of the battery, and the black lead to the negative (-) post of the battery. Set the scale of the voltmeter to read battery voltage. Turn the headlights on for 1 minute to remove the surface charge. Turn off the headlights and read the voltmeter.

Step #1 - **Battery Voltage:** 12.6 volts or higher = 100% charged
                        12.4 volts   = 75% charged
                        12.2 volts   = 50% charged
                        12.0 volts   = 25% charged

Battery Voltage_____ OK____ NOT OK____

Step #2 - **Cranking Voltage:** Disable the ignition or hold the accelerator to the floor on a fuel injection system to prevent the engine from starting. While cranking the engine with the ignition key, observe the voltmeter. The voltage should be above 9.6 volts.

Cranking Voltage_____ OK____ NOT OK____

If at or below 9.6 volts, there is a possible problem with:
   a. defective (or dirty) battery cables and connections.
   b. defective (or discharged) battery (under load).
   c. defective starter, solenoid or relay.

Step #3 - **Charging Voltage:** Reconnect the coil wire and start the engine. With the engine running at approximately 2,000 RPM (fast idle), the voltage should be 13.5-15 volts (or a minimum 1/2 volt higher than battery voltage and a maximum of 2 volts higher than battery voltage).

Charging Voltage_____ OK____ NOT OK____

If over 15 volts, there is a possible defective voltage regulator or connections. If under 13.5 volts (or under 1/2 volt over battery voltage), there is a possible problem with:
   a. loose drive belt.   c. defective voltage regulator.
   b. defective generator.   d. dirty or defective wiring connections.

48

Starter Current Draw Test

Meets NATEF Task: (A6-C-1) Perform starter current draw tests; determine necessary action.
(P-1)

Name _____ Date _____ Time on Task _____

Make/Model/Year _____ VIN _____ Evaluation: 4 3 2 1

_____ **1.** Connect the starting and charging test leads (such as a Sun Electric VAT-40) as per the manufacturer's instructions.

_____ **2.** Disable the ignition system or the fuel system to prevent the engine from starting.

_____ **3.** Crank the engine observing the ammeter scale (disregard the initial higher amp reading).

_____ **4.** Starter amperage specifications for this vehicle = _____ amps.

        4-cylinder engine = 150 to 185 amperes
        6-cylinder engine = 160 to 200 amperes
        8-cylinder engine = 185 to 250 amperes

_____ **5.** Starter amperage test results = _____ amps.

        OK_____   **NOT OK**_____

HINT: If the amperage reading is higher than the maximum allowable, double check the battery condition before removing the starter motor for disassembly, testing, or replacement. An engine problem can also cause an excessive amperage reading. If the amperage reading is within specifications (less than the maximum allowable), yet the starter motor is operating slowly, check for excessive resistance in the battery cables.

49

Generator (Alternator) Output Test

Meets NATEF Task: (A6-D-1) Perform charging system output test; determine necessary action. (P-1)

Name _____ Date _____ Time on Task _____

Make/Model/Year _____ VIN _____ Evaluation: 4 3 2 1

_____ **1.** Connect the starting and charging test unit (such as a Sun VAT-40) leads as per the manufacturer's instructions.

_____

_____

_____ **2.** Start the engine and operate at 2,000 RPM (fast idle).

_____ **3.** Turn the "load increase" control slowly to obtain the highest reading on the ammeter scale. (Do not let the battery voltage drop to less than 13 volts.)
Tested amps = _____ amps.

_____ **4.** Check service information for the output specification (should be stamped on the generator (alternator) or indicated by a colored tag on or near the output terminal) = _____ amps.

_____ **5.** Results should be within 10% of the specifications. If the generator amperage output is low, first check the condition of the generator drive belt. It should not be possible to
rotate the generator by hand with the engine "off."

OK_____   **NOT OK**_____

_____ **6.** Based on the test, what is the necessary action? _____

_____

50

Distributor Cap and Rotor

Meets NATEF Task: (A8-C-2) Inspect and test ignition primary and secondary circuit wiring and solid state components; test ignition coil(s); perform necessary action. (P-1)

Name _____ Date _____ Time on Task _____

Make/Model/Year _____ VIN _____ Evaluation: 4 3 2 1

_____ 1. Check service information for the specified items to inspect and test in the secondary ignition circuit.

_____

_____ 2. Carefully remove the distributor cap (the spark plug wires do not have to be removed from the cap).

_____ 3. Determine the **locating tab** on the distributor cap.

_____ 4. Check the **towers** for corrosion by removing one spark wire from the cap at a time.

_____ 5. Check the **center carbon insert** for chips or cracks.

_____ 6. Check the **side inserts** inside the cap for excessive corrosion and dusting.

_____ 7. Check the cap for **cracks** or **carbon tracks** inside and out.

_____ 8. Check the condition of the **rotor**.

   OK _____   NOT OK _____

_____ 9. Based on the inspection, what is the necessary action?

_____

_____

51

Spark Plugs

Meets NATEF Task: (A8-C-2) Inspect and test ignition primary and secondary circuit wiring and solid state components; test ignition coil(s); perform necessary action. (P-1)

Name _____ Date _____ Time on Task _____

Make/Model/Year _____ VIN _____ Evaluation: 4 3 2 1

_____ **1.** Determine the correct plug code and gap for your vehicle using a spark plug application guide.

ENGINE: #cylinders_____ VIN# _____

BRAND _____ CODE# _____ GAP _____

_____ **2.** Remove all of the spark plugs and label all the spark plug wires.

_____ **3.** Determine the condition and gap of all spark plugs:

	Condition	**Gap**
1.	_____	_____
2.	_____	_____
3.	_____	_____
4.	_____	_____
5.	_____	_____
6.	_____	_____
7.	_____	_____
8.	_____	_____

_____ **4.** Reinstall the spark plug (start by hand).

_____ **5.** Use a torque wrench and torque the spark plugs to the proper torque.

Specified torque = _____

_____ **6.** Start the engine. Check for possible rough running caused by crossed or loose spark plug wires.

OK_____ NOT OK_____

52

We Support
NATEF

Spark Plug Wires

Meets NATEF Task: (A8-C-2) Inspect and test ignition primary and secondary circuit wiring and solid state components; test ignition coil(s); perform necessary action. (P-1)

Name _____ Date _____ Time on Task _____

Make/Model/Year _____ VIN _____ Evaluation: 4 3 2 1

_____ **1.** Check service information to determine the specified spark plug wire resistance specification.

_____

_____ **2.** Set the digital multimeter to read ohms (Ω). (200 k if normal range meter)

_____ **3.** Carefully disconnect both ends of a spark plug wire (there is no need to remove the wire if both ends can be reached).

_____ **4.** List the length in feet and the resistance values in ohms for each spark plug wire according to the cylinder number:

Length (feet)	Ohms
1. _____	_____
2. _____	_____
3. _____	_____
4. _____	_____
5. _____	_____
6. _____	_____
7. _____	_____
8. _____	_____

OHMMETER

DISTRIBUTOR CAP

OMMETER LEADS

PLUG CABLE

Coil wire (if equipped): _____ _____

_____ **5.** Results - Usually 10,000 ohms (10 kΩ) or *less* per foot of length.

OK_____   NOT OK_____

53

Ignition Timing

Meets NATEF Task: (Not specified by NATEF)

Name _____ **Date** _____ **Time on Task** _____

Make/Model/Year _____ **VIN** _____ **Evaluation: 4   3   2   1**

Specifications:

_____ **1.** Timing *specifications*: _____BTDC at _____RPM.

_____ **2.** According to a service manual, what had to be done before checking the ignition timing? _____

Hook-Up and Procedure:

_____ **3.** Connect the power to the timing light according to the manufacturer's directions (usually to + and - of the battery).

_____ **4.** Hook the inductive pickup to the #1 cylinder near the distributor.

_____ **5.** Chalk the timing marks.

_____ **6.** Remove and plug the vacuum hose at the distributor, if required. Computer-equipped engines require exact timing procedures. Consult the underhood decal for timing information.

_____ **7.** The engine should be warm and at the correct timing RPM.

_____ **8.** Timing was at _____   **OK** _____   **NOT OK** _____

_____ **9.** If the timing is incorrect, loosen the nut at the bottom of the distributor (base) and rotate the distributor until the timing marks line up.

_____ **10.** Tighten the distributor hold-down and recheck the timing.

_____ **11.** Reinstall the vacuum lines or set timing connections.

54

Exhaust Gas Analysis

Meets NATEF Task: (A8-A-13) Prepare 4 or 5 gas analyzer; inspect and prepare vehicle for test, and obtain exhaust readings; interpret readings, and determine necessary action. (P-3)

Name _____ Date _____ Time on Task _____

Make/Model/Year _____ VIN _____ Evaluation: 4 3 2 1

_____ **1.** Check the instruction information for the exhaust gas analyzer being used to determine the proper test procedures to follow.

_____

_____

_____ **2.** Check the vehicle for exhaust leaks and other faults that could affect the exhaust gas readings.

_____

_____ **3.** Prepare the vehicle for testing, which usually includes operating the engine until normal operating temperature has been achieved. List other items listed by the test equipment manufacturer that should be performed.

_____

_____

_____ **4.** Obtain the exhaust gas readings and compare them to specifications.

Gas	Idle	2500 RPM	General Specifications
HC			Max 50 PPM
CO			Max 0.5%
CO_2			12% to 15% or higher
O_2			0% to 2%
NO_X			Less than 100 PPM @ idle Less than 1000 PPM @ wide open throttle

_____ **5.** Based on the exhaust gas readings, what is the necessary action?

_____

55

Diagnosis of Emission-Related Concerns

Meets NATEF Task: (A8-B-2) Diagnose the causes of emissions or driveability concerns resulting from malfunctions in the computerized engine control system with stored diagnostic trouble codes. (P-1)

Name _____ Date _____ Time on Task _____

Make/Model/Year _____ VIN _____ Evaluation: 4 3 2 1

_____ **1.** Check service information for the specified methods to follow to determine the cause of an emission-related concern with stored diagnostic trouble codes.

_____

_____

_____

_____

_____

_____ **2.** Following the vehicle manufacturer's recommended procedure, retrieve the stored DTC(s).

DTC	Description of DTC	Possible Causes

_____ **3.** What emission concerns could result from faults indicated by the DTCs?

_____

_____

_____ **4.** Based on the test results and service information, what is the necessary action?

_____

56

We Support
NATEF

Exhaust System Backpressure Test

Meets NATEF Task: (A8-D-9) Perform exhaust system backpressure test; determine necessary action. (P-1)

Name _____ **Date** _____ **Time on Task** _____

Make/Model/Year _____ **VIN** _____ **Evaluation:** 4 3 2 1

A clogged or partially restricted exhaust greatly affects engine performance. Lack of power is a common symptom of a partially restricted exhaust system. In severe cases, the engine may start/stall due to exhaust system restriction.

_____ **1.** Check service information for the specified maximum backpressure. _____

_____

_____ **2.** Remove the oxygen sensor from the exhaust manifold and install tool to measure exhaust back pressure.

NOTE: This tool can be made from an 18 mm fitting and a vacuum hose nipple.

_____ **3.** Connect a vacuum/pressure gauge to the exhaust back pressure tool. Start the engine and run at idle and observe exhaust back pressure.

_____ psi back pressure (maximum allowable back pressure at idle is 1.25 psi.)

OK _____   NOT OK _____

_____ **4.** Operate the engine at a constant speed of 2500 RPM and observe the exhaust back pressure.

_____ psi back pressure (Maximum allowable back pressure at 2500 RPM is 2.5 psi.)

OK _____   NOT OK _____

_____ **5.** Based on the results of the backpressure test, what is the necessary action?

_____

57

We Support
NATEF

PCV System Diagnosis

Meets NATEF Task: (A8-E-1) Diagnose oil leaks, emissions, and driveability concerns caused by the positive crankcase ventilation (PCV) system; determine necessary action. (P-2)

Name _____ Date _____ Time on Task _____

Make/Model/Year _____ VIN _____ Evaluation: 4 3 2 1

_____ **1.** Check service information for the recommended procedures to follow when diagnosing the PCV system.

_____

_____

_____ **2.** Start the engine and allow it to idle and remove the oil fill cap.

_____ **3.** Place a piece of paper or a 3" x 5" card over the filler. (The PCV system is functioning correctly if the paper is held down tight onto the filler by vacuum in the crankcase).

_____ **4.** Seal off the oil fill opening and measure the crankcase vacuum at the dipstick tube = _____ (should be about 0.5 in. Hg. or 7 in. or more of water if using a water manometer).

OK _____   NOT OK _____

_____ **5.** Based on the test results, what is the necessary action?

_____

_____

_____

58

We Support NATEF

PCV System Inspection

Meets NATEF Task: (A8-E-1-2) Inspect, test and service PCV hoses, tubes and filter; perform necessary action. (P-2)

Name _____ Date _____ Time on Task _____

Make/Model/Year _____ VIN _____ Evaluation: 4 3 2 1

_____ 1. Check service information for the recommended steps to follow when testing or servicing the positive crankcase ventilation (PCV) system.

_____

_____

_____ 2. Check service information and describe the location of the following:

PCV valve _____

Crankcase vent filter _____

Fixed orifice (if equipped) _____

Other (describe) _____

_____ 3. What is specified replacement interval for the PCV valve?

_____

_____ 4. Remove and clear the PCV valve (if equipped) and note the condition.

_____ Like new   _____ Very dirty

_____ Slightly dirty   _____ Valve clogged or stuck

_____ Other (describe) _____

_____ 5. Based on the test and inspection and on the recommendation of the vehicle manufacturer, what is the necessary action?

_____

59

We Support
ASE NATEF

PCV System Test

Meets NATEF Task: (A8-E-2) Inspect, test and service PCV hoses, tubes and filter; perform necessary action. (P-2)

Name _____ Date _____ Time on Task _____

Make/Model/Year _____ VIN _____ Evaluation: 4 3 2 1

The purpose of the "positive crankcase ventilation" (PCV) system is to use engine intake manifold vacuum to draw crankcase vapors that occur due to blow-by past the piston rings into the engine to be burned.

NOTE: If there is gasoline in the engine oil, gasoline vapors will be drawn into the engine and the intake charge will be richer. Therefore, if black exhaust smoke or a rich condition is being diagnosed, check the crankcase for the presence of gasoline.

A good PCV system should draw fresh air into the engine through a filter usually located in the air cleaner or on the valve (cam) cover. This filtered air then is mixed with the blow-by gases in the crankcase and through a PCV valve which regulates the flow into the engine.

PCV Valve Operation:

a. Idle = high vacuum = PCV valve almost closed by high vacuum.

b. At cruise = 10-15 in. Hg. = PCV valve is opened to allow the crankcase gases to be drawn into the engine (vacuum and internal spring are almost balanced).

c. At wide open throttle (WOT) low vacuum = PCV valve is fully opened by internal spring permitting maximum flow.

Testing the System:

_____ 1. Start the engine and allow it to idle.

_____ 2. Remove the oil fill cap.

_____ 3. Place a piece of paper or a 3" x 5" card over the filler. (The PCV system is functioning correctly if the paper is held down tight onto the filler by vacuum in the crankcase).

_____ 4. Seal off the oil fill opening and measure the crankcase vacuum at the dipstick tube = _____ (should be about 0.5 in. Hg. or 7 in. or more of water if using a water manometer).
         OK _____   NOT OK _____

60

EGR System Diagnosis

Meets NATEF Task: (A8-E-3) Diagnose emission and driveability problems caused by malfunctions in the exhaust gas recirculation (EGR) system; determining necessary action. (P-1)

Name _____ Date _____ Time on Task _____

Make/Model/Year _____ VIN _____ Evaluation: 4 3 2 1

The purpose and function of the exhaust gas recirculation (EGR) valve is to blend a slight amount (about 7%) of exhaust gas into the fresh intake charge entering the combustion chamber. The burned exhaust gases are inert and therefore, cannot react chemically with the burning process. The exhaust gases take up mass in the combustion chamber and slow the burning of the air/fuel mixture reducing the peak temperatures that would normally occur if the exhaust gases were not present. This prevents combustion chamber temperatures from exceeding 2500°F (1370°C) and reduces the formation of oxides of nitrogen (NO_X) exhaust emissions.

A typical EGR problem:

- Too much EGR flow causes rough idle and stalling (engine could operate okay at highway speeds).

- Too little EGR flow causes spark knock (ping or detonation) and excessive NO_X emissions especially during cruise and moderate acceleration.

_____ 1. Check service information for the specified procedures to follow when diagnosing the EGR system.

_____ 2. Based on the test, what is the necessary action?

_____

_____

_____

_____

61

Ford Pressure Feedback EGR (PFE)

Meets NATEF Task: (A8-E-4) Diagnose emissions and driveability problems caused by malfunctions in the EGR system; determine necessary action. (P-1)

Name _____ Date _____ Time on Task _____

Make/Model/Year _____ VIN _____ Evaluation: 4   3   2   1

Exhaust back pressure is used to control the amount of exhaust gas recirculation (EGR). The EGR valve is normally closed at both idle and wide open throttle (WOT). The EGR vacuum regulator (EVR) solenoid is pulsed on and off to give the ideal amount of EGR flow for a given back pressure.

Back Pressure	Voltage
0 psi	3.25
0.5 psi	3.66
0.75 psi	3.78
1.0 psi	4.08
1.25 psi	4.28
1.50 psi	4.50
1.80 psi	4.75

_____ **1.** Check service information for the specified procedures for testing the Ford pressure feedback EGR.

_____

_____

_____ **2.** Voltage at idle = _____ volts (should be 3.25 V)

  OK _____   NOT OK _____

_____ **3.** Voltage at steady speed (50 mph) = _____ volts (should be 3.4 to 3.8 V).

  OK _____   NOT OK _____

_____ **4.** Based on the test results, what is the necessary action?

62

Service EGR System

Meets NATEF Task: (A8-E-4) Inspect, test, and service components of the EGR system; perform necessary action. (P-1)

Name _____ Date _____ Time on Task _____

Make/Model/Year _____ VIN _____ Evaluation: 4 3 2 1

The EGR passages and valve that control the flow of exhaust gases can become clogged with carbon. The EGR valve and passages may need to be cleaned if one or more of the following conditions are present.

- A computer diagnosis trouble code (DTC) indicating the lack of EGR flow
- The failure of an exhaust emission test for excessive NOx
- Excessive engine spark knock (ping or detonation)

_____ 1. Check service information for the recommended procedures to follow when servicing the EGR system.

_____

_____ 2. What problem(s) exists? _____

_____ 3. Remove the EGR valve and inspect for clogged passages. Clean as needed.

Valve was clogged _____   Valve was OK _____

_____ 4. Start the engine. Exhaust should be heard and felt coming from the open passage where the EGR valve was located.

CAUTION: Be sure to wear eye protection. Particles of carbon can be forced out of the EGR passage with great force when the engine starts.

Exhaust flowed freely _____   Exhaust did not flow freely _____

_____ 5. To clean the passages of carbon, remove the plugs or EGR valve and insert a stiff wire into an electric drill and use it to ream out the passages.

_____ 6. Reinstall the EGR valve with a new gasket and check the engine for proper operation.

_____ 7. What is the necessary action? _____

_____

63

EGR System Scan Tool Diagnosis

Meets NATEF Task: (A8-E-4) Inspect, test, service and replace the EGR system, including EGR tubing, exhaust passages, vacuum/pressure controls, filters, hoses; perform necessary action. (P-1)

Name _____ Date _____ Time on Task _____

Make/Model/Year _____ VIN _____ Evaluation: 4 3 2 1

_____ 1. Check service information for the specified testing procedure of the exhaust gas recirculation (EGR) system using a scan tool.

_____

_____

_____ 2. List the EGR-related data that can be retrieved using a scan tool.

_____

_____ 3. List the scan tool commands (bi-directional) for the EGR system and describe the results of the tests.

Unit Commanded	Results
_____	_____
_____	_____
_____	_____

_____ 4. Has the EGR OBD II monitor run? _____

_____ 5. Based on the results of the scan tool diagnosis, what is the necessary action?

_____

_____

_____

_____

64

EGR Electrical Sensors

Meets NATEF Task: (A8-E-5) Inspect and test electrical/electronic sensors, controls and wiring of the exhaust gas recirculation system; perform necessary action. (P-2)

Name _____ Date _____ Time on Task _____

Make/Model/Year _____ VIN _____ Evaluation: 4 3 2 1

_____ **1.** Check service information for the recommended tests and diagnostic procedure to follow to diagnose EGR system sensors and controls.

_____

_____

_____

_____

_____

_____ **2.** List the tools and equipment needed as specified by the vehicle manufacturer. Check all that apply.

_____ Scan tool

_____ Vacuum pump

_____ Digital multimeter (DMM)

_____ 5-gas exhaust analyzer

_____ Other (describe) _____

_____ **3.** Based on the test results, what is the necessary action?

_____

_____

65

We Support
ASE NATEF

Ford EVP Voltage Check

Meets NATEF Task: (A8-E-5) Inspect and test electrical/electronic sensors, controls and wiring of the EGR system; perform necessary action. (P-2)

Name _____ Date _____ Time on Task _____

Make/Model/Year _____ VIN _____ Evaluation: 4 3 2 1

The EGR valve position (EVP) sensor is used by the PCM to provide feedback as to the actual position of the EGR valve. If the actual position and the commanded position are different, a diagnostic trouble code could be set. An EVP signal that is out-of-range can also cause an incorrect fuel mixture to be supplied to the engine. Compare the voltage reading to the percentage of EGR valve opening.

- Check that the valve is able to be fully closed (could be stuck with carbon).

- If the EVP is too low, ignition timing will be retarded.

_____ **1.** Check service information for the exact specification for the vehicle being tested (typical specification).

EGR Opening Percentage	Black Sensor Volts	Gray Sensor Volts
0%	0.90	0.35
10%	1.25	0.75
20%	1.65	1.10
30%	1.95	1.45
40%	2.30	1.80
50%	2.65	2.15
60%	3.00	2.50
70%	3.35	2.85
80%	3.70	3.20
90%	4.05	3.55
100%	4.40	3.90

_____ **2.** Does the voltage and the commanded position as determined by a scan tool agree?

Yes _____ No _____

_____ **3.** Based on the test results, what is the necessary action? _____

Secondary Air Injection Diagnosis

Meets NATEF Task: (A8-E-6) Diagnose emission and driveability problems resulting from malfunctions in the secondary air injection system; determine necessary action. (P-2)

Name _____ Date _____ Time on Task _____

Make/Model/Year _____ VIN _____ Evaluation: 4 3 2 1

AIR means "air injection reaction." An AIR pump supplies additional air to the exhaust system to reduce carbon monoxide (CO) and unburned gasoline (hydrocarbons or HC) exhaust emissions. Most AIR pump systems supply air to the exhaust manifold (exhaust ports) until the engine reaches closed loop operation. As soon as the computer reaches closed loop, the air flow is directed to the catalytic converter to help the catalyst oxidize the HC and CO into harmless water (H_2O) and carbon dioxide (CO_2).

_____ 1. Check service information for the recommended test procedure and specifications for the secondary air injection system.

_____

_____

COLD ENGINE
BYPASS DIVERTER VALVE (SOLENOID)
CHECK VALVE
ELECTRICAL SIGNALS FROM THE COMPUTER
CHECK VALVE
EXHAUST MANIFOLD
CATALYTIC CONVERTER
(a)

_____ 2. Locate the air pump.

_____ 3. Carefully inspect the condition of all of the hoses, check the valves and the metal lines for corrosion or damage.

HOT ENGINE
BYPASS DIVERTER VALVE (SOLENOID)
CHECK VALVE
ELECTRICAL SIGNALS FROM THE COMPUTER
CHECK VALVE
EXHAUST MANIFOLD
CATALYTIC CONVERTER
(b)

_____ 4. Start the engine and feel the air pump lines to confirm the proper air flow.

NOTE: A defective one-way check valve at the exhaust manifold can allow hot exhaust gases to flow past the check valve and cause damage to the switching valves, hoses or air pump itself. These exhaust gases can cause poor engine operation and stalling if drawn into the air intake system.

_____ 5. Inspect the air pump drive belt for cracks and proper tension or electrical connections for an electric air pump.

_____ 6. Based on the inspection and test results, what is the necessary action?

_____

67

AIR Pump Component Inspection

Meets NATEF Task: (A8-E-7) Inspect and test mechanical components of the secondary air injection system; perform necessary action. (P-3)

Name _____ **Date** _____ **Time on Task** _____

Make/Model/Year _____ **VIN** _____ **Evaluation:** 4   3   2   1

_____ **1.** Check service information for the recommended procedures to follow when inspecting and testing the AIR pump components.

_____

_____ **2.** Carefully inspect the condition of all of the hoses, check the valves and the metal lines for corrosion or damage.

_____ **3.** Start the engine and feel the air pump lines to confirm the proper air flow.

NOTE: A defective one-way check valve at the exhaust manifold can allow hot exhaust gases to flow past the check valve and cause damage to the switching valves, hoses or air pump itself. These exhaust gases can cause poor engine operation and stalling if drawn into the air intake system.

_____ **4.** Inspect the air pump drive belt for cracks and proper tension.

_____ **5.** Based on the inspection, what is the necessary action?

_____

_____

_____

68

We Support
NATEF

AIR Pump Component Inspection

Meets NATEF Task: (A8-E-7) Inspect and test mechanical components of the secondary air injection system; perform necessary action. (P-3)

Name _____ Date _____ Time on Task _____

Make/Model/Year _____ VIN _____ Evaluation: 4 3 2 1

_____ **1.** Check service information for the recommended procedures to follow when inspecting and testing the AIR pump components.

_____

_____ **2.** Carefully inspect the condition of all of the hoses, check the valves and the metal lines for corrosion or damage.

_____ **3.** Start the engine and feel the air pump lines to confirm the proper air flow.

NOTE: A defective one-way check valve at the exhaust manifold can allow hot exhaust gases to flow past the check valve and cause damage to the switching valves, hoses or air pump itself. These exhaust gases can cause poor engine operation and stalling if drawn into the air intake system.

_____ **4.** Inspect the air pump drive belt for cracks and proper tension.

_____ **5.** Based on the inspection, what is the necessary action?

_____

_____

_____

69

Catalytic Converter Test

Meets NATEF Task: (A8-E-9) Inspect and test catalytic converter efficiency.
(P-1)

Name _____ Date _____ Time on Task _____

Make/Model/Year _____ VIN _____ Evaluation: 4 3 2 1

_____ **1.** Check service information for the recommended test to perform on the catalytic converter.

_____

_____

_____ **2.** The recommended test(s) include the following. Check all that apply.

_____ Check for loose substrate (rattle noise)

_____ Check temperature differences

_____ Use propane

_____ Use an exhaust gas analyzer

_____ Other (describe) _____

_____ **3.** Which tests were performed and what were the results?

a. _____ Result: _____

b. _____ Result: _____

c. _____ Result: _____

_____ **4.** Based on the tests and inspection of the catalytic converter, what is the necessary action?

_____

_____

70

Catalytic Converter Rattle Test

Meets NATEF Task: (A8-E-9 Inspect and test catalytic converter efficiency.
(P-1)

Name _____ Date _____ Time on Task _____

Make/Model/Year _____ VIN _____ Evaluation: 4 3 2 1

_____ **1.** Safely hoist the vehicle.

_____ **2.** Using your fist or a small rubber mallet, lightly tap on the catalytic converter. If the

converter rattles, it is broken internally and requires replacement.

> **NOTE:** If the catalytic converter has broken substrate, the muffler may also
> require replacement.

_____ **3.** Based on the results of this test, what is the necessary action? _____

_____

71

Catalytic Converter Performance Test

Meets NATEF Task: (A8-E-9) Inspect and test catalytic converter efficiency.
(P-1)

Name _____ **Date** _____ **Time on Task** _____

Make/Model/Year _____ **VIN** _____ **Evaluation:** 4 3 2 1

(Temperature Difference)

A catalytic converter uses a catalyst to start a chemical reaction, but does not enter into the chemical reaction. Because a chemical reaction causes heat, the temperature of the catalytic converter should be at least 10% hotter at the outlet as compared to the temperature of the inlet.

_____ 1. Start the engine and run at a fast idle (2500 RPM) for at least 2 minutes to fully warm up the oxygen sensor, the engine coolant and catalytic converter.

_____ 2. Using a pyrometer (infrared or contact type), measure the front (inlet) and outlet of the catalytic converter.

Inlet temperature = _____°

Outlet temperature = _____°

Difference = _____°

_____ 3. Results: If the outlet temperature is 50°F (10°C) (or 10%) higher than the inlet temperature, the catalytic converter is functioning correctly. **OK** ___ **NOT OK** ___

NOTE: Some engines are operating so cleanly that the catalytic converter has limited emissions to convert and therefore, the temperature of the converter may not show an increase in temperature. To check if the catalytic converter is functioning on a vehicle with very low exhaust emissions, simply use a vacuum hose connected to a spark plug wire and temporarily ground out one cylinder by using a tester light or jumper wire attached to ground. Measure the inlet and outlet temperatures of the converter while one cylinder is grounded out. To avoid damage to the catalytic converter, do not ground out a cylinder for longer than 10 seconds.

_____ 4. Based on the test results, what is the necessary action? _____

_____

72

Evaporative Emission Controls Diagnosis

Meets NATEF Task: (A8-E-11) Inspect and test components and hoses of the evaporative emissions control system; perform necessary action. (P-1)

Name _____ **Date** _____ **Time on Task** _____

Make/Model/Year _____ **VIN** _____ **Evaluation: 4   3   2   1**

_____ **1.** Check service information for the specified tests and procedures to follow to diagnose the problems in the evaporative emission control system.

_____

_____

_____

_____ **2.** List the tools and equipment specified for use by service information. Check all that apply.

_____ Special tester (describe) _____

_____ Scan tool

_____ Other (describe) _____

_____ **3.** List the components included in the evaporative emission control unit and describe how each is to be tested according to service information.

Component	Test or Inspection
a. _____	_____
b. _____	_____
c. _____	_____
d. _____	_____

_____ **4.** Based on the results of the tests and inspection, what is the necessary action?

_____

73

EVAP System Scan Tool Testing

Meets NATEF Task: (A8-E-11) Inspect and test components and hoses of the evaporative emissions control system; perform necessary action. (P-1)

***

Name _____ **Date** _____ **Time on Task** _____

Make/Model/Year _____ **VIN** _____ **Evaluation: 4   3   2   1**

_____ **1.** Check service information for the recommended checks and test procedures to follow when diagnosing the EVAP system using a scan tool.

_____

_____

_____ **2.** List the solenoids that can be commanded on or off using a scan tool. (Note: The factory scan tool or an enhanced version of an aftermarket scan tool may be necessary to provide bi-directional control of the components in the EVAP system.)

Component	Command ON/Off?
_____	_____
_____	_____
_____	_____
_____	_____

_____ **3.** Using the scan tool, what EVAP-related data (PID) is displayed?

PID	Value Displayed
_____	_____
_____	_____
_____	_____
_____	_____

_____ **4.** Based on the test results using a scan tool, what is the necessary action? _____

_____

74

Canister Purge Flow Rate Test

Meets NATEF Task: (A8-E-11) Inspect and test components and hoses of the evaporative emissions control system; perform necessary action. (P-1)

Name _____ Date _____ Time on Task _____

Make/Model/Year _____ VIN _____ Evaluation: 4 3 2 1

_____ **1.** Check service information for the purge flow rate specifications and test procedures.

_____

_____

Purge flow rate (usually a minimum of one liter per minute) = _____

When does purge occur? _____

_____ **2.** Convert the designated purge flow rate gauge to the charcoal canister following the instructions of the tester.

_____

Purge flow rate = _____ liters per minute

____ **OK** ____ **NOT OK**

_____ **3.** Based on the purge flow test results, what is the necessary action? _____

_____

_____

_____

RUBBER HOSE

CLEAR PLASTIC FLOW GAUGE

LOCATION OF STEEL BALL INDICATES AMOUNT OF CANISTER PURGE IN LITERS PER MINUTE

TO MANIFOLD

RUBBER HOSE

CHARCOAL CANISTER

75

EVAP System Component Inspection

Meet NATEF Task: (A8-E-11) Inspect and test components and hoses of the evaporative emissions control system; perform necessary action. (P-1)

Name _____ **Date** _____ **Time on Task** _____

Make/Model/Year _____ **VIN** _____ **Evaluation:** 4 3 2 1

_____ **1.** According to the underhood emission label, with what type of system is the vehicle equipped?

   _____ Pre-OBD I (1987 or older)

   _____ OBD I (1988-1995)

   _____ OBD II (1996 and newer)

   _____ Unknown (describe) _____

_____ **2.** Check the service information and the vehicle emission label for the following information.

  a. The location of the carbon canister
  (describe) _____

  _____

  b. The location of the purge control
  solenoid(s) (describe) _____

  _____

  c. The resistance specification for the evaporator control solenoid(s) = _____

_____ **3.** Visually inspect the following items and check for any sign of a leak in the system.

  a. Canister hoses **OK** _____ **NOT OK** _____

  b. Gas cap   **OK** _____ **NOT OK** _____

_____ **4.** Based on the inspection, what is the necessary action?

  _____

  _____

76

Smoke Test of the EVAP System

Meets NATEF Task: (A8-E-1) Inspect and test components and hoses of the evaporative emissions control system; perform necessary action. (P-1)

Name _____ Date _____ Time on Task _____

Make/Model/Year _____ VIN _____ Evaluation: 4 3 2 1

_____ 1. Check service information for the procedures and pressures to follow when checking the evaporative emission control system for leaks using smoke.

_____

_____

Specified maximum pressure = _____

_____ 2. Connect the smoke machine to the evaporative emission control system following the instructions supplied with the smoke machine.

_____

_____

_____

_____

_____ 3. Use a bright light and look for smoke leaking from the evaporative emission control system. Describe the leaks, if any.

_____

_____

_____ 4. Based on the results of the smoke testing, what is the necessary action? _____

_____

77

Evaporative Emission DTC Diagnosis

Meets NATEF Task: (A8-E-11) Inspect and test components and hoses of the evaporative emissions control system; perform necessary action. (P-1)

Name _____ Date _____ Time on Task _____

Make/Model/Year _____ VIN _____ Evaluation: 4 3 2 1

_____ **1.** Check service information for the specified diagnostic steps to follow if evaporative emission control-related DTC(s) is set.

_____

_____

_____ **2.** Describe the test and inspection specified for each of the DTCs listed.

DTC	Specified Test(s)
P0440	_____
P0441	_____
P0442	_____
Other (list)	_____
Other (list)	_____

_____ **3.** Based on the results of the tests and inspection, what is the necessary action?

_____

_____

_____

78

Port Fuel-Injection Intake Manifold Identification

Meets NATEF Task: Not specified by NATEF

Name _____ **Date** _____ **Time on Task** _____

Make/Model/Year _____ **VIN** _____ **Evaluation:** 4 3 2 1

_____ **1.** The intake manifold (plenum) is a:

     _____ one-piece design

     _____ two-piece design

     _____ more than two pieces

_____ **2.** The manifold (plenum) is constructed of:

     _____ plastic

     _____ aluminum

     _____ composite (more than one material)

_____ **3.** The engine has:

     _____ one intake valve per cylinder

     _____ two intake valves per cylinder

     _____ three intake valves per cylinder

_____ **4.** The throttle body is:

     _____ a separate replaceable part

     _____ part of the intake manifold

_____ **5.** The manifold includes a manifold tuning valve.

     _____ **Yes**

     _____ **No**

_____ **6.** The fuel rails for the injector are:

     _____ plastic

     _____ metal

79

Exhaust Manifold Identification

Meets NATEF Task: Not specified by NATEF

Name _____ Date _____ Time on Task _____

Make/Model/Year _____ VIN _____ Evaluation: 4 3 2 1

_____ **1.** Number of exhaust manifolds on the engine?

        _____ one
        _____ two

_____ **2.** Type of material used?

        _____ cast iron
        _____ steel (header-type manifold)
        _____ other (describe)

_____

_____ **3.** Exhaust manifold(s) laminated (two pieces sandwiched together)?

        Yes _____ No _____

_____ **4.** Is there a gasket used between the exhaust manifold and the cylinder head from the factory?

        Yes _____ No _____

_____ **5.** What type of fasteners are used to hold the exhaust manifold to the cylinder head?

        _____ bolts
        _____ nuts (uses studs in the head)

_____ **6.** What is the torque specification for the fasteners?

_____

_____ **7.** Carefully inspect the exhaust manifold for cracks or damage.

        OK ____ **NOT OK** ____

80

Exhaust System Inspection

Meets NATEF Task: Not specified by NATEF

Name _____ **Date** _____ **Time on Task** _____

Make/Model/Year _____ **VIN** _____ **Evaluation:** 4 3 2 1

_____ **1.** Safely hoist the vehicle and wear safety glasses.

_____ **2.** Visually inspect the following items and note their condition.

Tailpipe **OK** _____ **NOT OK** _____
Describe fault: _____

Muffler **OK** _____ **NOT OK** _____
Describe fault: _____

Exhaust Pipe **OK** _____ **NOT OK** _____
Describe fault: _____

Hangers **OK** _____ **NOT OK** _____
Describe fault: _____

Catalytic converter **OK** _____ **NOT OK** _____
Describe fault: _____

Header or Y-pipe **OK** _____ **NOT OK** _____
Describe fault: _____

Exhaust manifold(s) **OK** _____ **NOT OK** _____
Describe fault: _____

Heat shields(s) **OK** _____ **NOT OK** _____
Describe fault: _____

Other (describe) _____
_____

_____ **3.** Based on the inspection, what is the necessary action? _____
_____

81

TBI/Carburetor Intake Manifold Identification

Meets NATEF Task: Not specified by NATEF

Name _____ **Date** _____ **Time on Task** _____

Make/Model/Year _____ **VIN** _____ **Evaluation:** 4 3 2 1

_____ **1.** The intake manifold is a:

      _____ one-piece design

      _____ two-piece design

      _____ more than two piece

_____ **2.** The manifold is constructed of:

      _____ plastic   _____ aluminum   _____ composite (more than one material)

_____ **3.** The engine uses:

      _____ one intake valve per cylinder

      _____ two intake valves per cylinder

_____ **4.** The intake manifold is equipped with an EGR valve or EGR passages.

      Yes _____   **No** _____

_____ **5.** How does the intake manifold heat the air/fuel mixture?

      _____ exhaust crossover passages

      _____ electrically heated grid under the TBI/carburetor

      _____ other (describe) _____

82

Intake Manifold Gasket Replacement

Meets NATEF Task: Not specified by NATEF

Name _____ Date _____ Time on Task _____

Make/Model/Year _____ VIN _____ Evaluation: 4   3   2   1

An intake manifold gasket will have to be replaced if there is one or more of the following problems:

- An air (vacuum) leak that affects the operation of the engine
- A coolant leak around the cooling passages of the intake manifold
- An oil leak from the gasket area of the intake manifold

_____ **1.** Check service information for the specified procedure and fastener torque specified. Describe the procedure. _____

_____

_____ **2.** Remove the intake manifold.

_____ **3.** Clean the gasket surfaces.

> **CAUTION:** Do not use fiber abrasive pads to clean the gasket surfaces. Particles of the fiber disc can get into the engine and cause serious engine wear and damage. Do not use steel tools to scrape gaskets from an aluminum surface.

_____ **4.** Install the replacement gasket(s) and the intake manifold. Torque the retaining bolts to factory specifications.

Intake manifold bolt torque specification = _____

_____ **5.** Reassemble the top of the engine.

_____ **6.** Refill the cooling system with new coolant.

> **CAUTION:** Be sure to open the cooling system bleeder valves(s), if equipped, to avoid trapping air.

_____ **7.** Install the radiator pressure cap and start the engine. Check for leaks and proper cooling system operation.

83

Turbocharger Identification

Meets NATEF Task: (A1-A-3) Research vehicle information. (P-1)

Name _____ **Date** _____ **Time on Task** _____

Make/Model/Year _____ **VIN** _____ **Evaluation:** 4 3 2 1

_____ **1.** Check service information and determine the following information:

    a. Location of the turbocharger (describe): _____

    _____

    b. Is the turbo system equipped with an intercooler? Yes _____ No _____

       If yes, describe the location and type (air-to-air or air-to-liquid) _____

    _____

    c. Type of turbocharger control includes (check all that apply):

      ___ 1. Wastegate

      ___ 2. Blow off valve

      ___ 3. Variable vane

    d. Are the turbocharger bushings liquid cooled? Yes _____ No _____

    e. What is the recommended oil change interval and specified engine oil?

      Recommended oil change interval: _____

      Recommended engine oil specification: _____

_____ **2.** Check turbocharger and verify that all components are free of defects, including hoses and hose clamps.

    OK _____   Not OK _____

    (describe faults) _____

    _____

    _____

    _____

84

Supercharger Identification

Meets NATEF Task: (A1-A-3) Research vehicle information. (P-1)

Name _____ Date _____ Time on Task _____

Make/Model/Year _____ VIN _____ Evaluation: 4 3 2 1

_____ **1.** Check service information and determine the following information:

    a. Location of supercharger: (describe) _____

      _____

    b. Type of boost control? (describe) _____

      _____

    c. Does the supercharger system use an intercooler? Yes ____ No ____

      If yes, describe the location and type (air-to-air or air-to-liquid): _____

      _____

    d. How is the supercharger unit lubricated? (describe) _____

      _____

    e. What is the recommended oil and oil change interval?

      Recommended oil _____

      Recommended oil change interval _____

_____ **2.** Check the supercharger and verify that all components are free from defects, including drive belt and hoses/clamps. **OK** _____ **Not OK** _____ If not OK, describe the faults: _____

_____

_____

_____

_____

_____

85

Test Operation of Turbocharger/Supercharger

Meets NATEF Task: (A8-D-10) Test the operation of turbocharger/supercharger systems; determine necessary action. (P-3)

Name _____ Date _____ Time on Task _____

Make/Model/Year _____ VIN _____ Evaluation: 4 3 2 1

_____ **1.** The vehicle is equipped with which system?

_____ Turbocharger (exhaust driven)

_____ Supercharger (engine driven)

_____ **2.** Check service information for the exact procedure to follow to determine the correct operation of the turbocharger/supercharger. Describe the inspection procedure.

_____

_____

_____

_____ **3.** Based on the specified test and inspection procedures, what is the necessary action?

_____

_____

_____

86

We Support
NATEF

Engine Problem Analysis

Meets NATEF Task: (A1-A-2) Identify and interpret engine concern; determine necessary action. (P-1)

Name _____ **Date** _____ **Time on Task** _____

Make/Model/Year _____ **VIN** _____ **Evaluation:** 4 3 2 1

_____ **1.** State the customer's concern regarding the engine problem. _____

_____

    A. Excessive noise? _____

    Describe: _____

    B. Exhaust smoke? _____

_____

    C. Engine operation (missing, runs rough, etc.)? Describe: _____

_____

_____ **2.** Based on the symptoms described above, what tests should be performed?

    ____ Compression test

    ____ Cylinder linkage test

    ____ Power balance test

    ____ Other (describe): _____

_____ **3.** Based on the symptoms and the test results, what is the necessary action?

_____

_____

_____

87

We Support
NATEF

Engine Noise Diagnosis

Meets NATEF Task: (A1-A-2) Identify and interpret engine concerns, determine necessary action (P-1)

___

Name _____ Date _____ Time on Task _____

Make/Model/Year _____ VIN _____ Evaluation: 4 3 2 1

Analyzing engine noise helps determine the extent of needed repairs. Some noises are easy to correct, whereas other noises may represent extensive and expensive repairs.

_____ 1. When does the noise occur?

      _____ at start up (cold engine only)

      _____ at start up (all the time)

      _____ cold engine only

      _____ warm engine only

      _____ all the time

      _____ other (describe)

_____

_____ 2. What does the noise sound like?

      _____ Clicking noise - like the clicking of a ballpoint pen

      _____ Clacking noise - like tapping on metal

      _____ Knock - like knocking on a door

      _____ Rattle - like a baby rattle

      _____ Clatter - like rolling marbles

      _____ Whine - like an electric motor running

      _____ Clunk - like a door closing

_____ 3. Based on the noise, what is the necessary action?

_____

_____

88

Fluid Leakage Detection

Meets NATEF Task: (A1-A-5) Inspect engine for fuel, oil, coolant and other leaks; determine necessary action (P-1)

Name _____ **Date** _____ **Time on Task** _____

Make/Model/Year _____ **VIN** _____ **Evaluation:** 4 3 2 1

_____ **1.** Check the fuel system for leaks from the fuel tank to the intake manifold.

      A. Visually check for leaks

          ____ OK – Nothing found visually

          ____ NOT OK – Found the leak – Describe the location: _____

          _____

      B. Smell test for leaks

          ____ OK – Did not smell fuel at any location

          ____ NOT OK – Smelled fuel – Describe the location: _____

          _____

      C. Hydrocarbon test for leaks

          ____ OK – Detector did not indicate any leaks

          ____ NOT OK – Fuel leak detected – Describe the location: _____

          _____

_____ **2.** Based on the inspection for fuel leaks, what is the necessary action? _____

_____

_____

89

Oil Leak Detection

Meets NATEF Task: (A1-A-5) Inspect engine for fuel, oil, coolant and other leaks; determine necessary action (P-1)

Name _____ Date _____ Time on Task _____

Make/Model/Year _____ VIN _____ Evaluation: 4 3 2 1

Engine oil is usually amber in color when new, but quickly becomes darker and often black when used in an engine. Before trying to repair an engine oil leak, make sure that the leak is actually engine oil and not some other fluid such as the following:

- **red** – automatic transmission fluid (also used in some power steering units)
- **green** – antifreeze coolant
- **orange** – antifreeze coolant
- **blue** – antifreeze coolant or windshield washer fluid
- **yellow** – windshield washer fluid
- **clear** – condensation from the air-conditioning system (normal)

_____ 1. Carefully inspect the areas where oil is likely to leak, including:

valve covers	OK _____	NOT OK _____
intake manifold area	OK _____	NOT OK _____
oil pressure-sending unit	OK _____	NOT OK _____

_____ 2. Safely hoist the vehicle and carefully inspect the underneath of the engine.

_____ 3. Where is the highest, most forward area of the leak? (describe) _____

_____

_____ 4. If the exact location cannot be located, lower the vehicle and add fluorescent dye to the engine oil. Drive the vehicle for 10 to 15 minutes and hoist the vehicle.

_____ 5. Using black light, locate the area of the leak by looking for the yellow/green areas highlighted by the dye. Describe the leak location:

_____

_____ 6. Based on the inspection for oil leaks, what is the necessary action? _____

_____

90

Coolant Leak Diagnosis

Meets NATEF Task: (A1-A-5) Inspect engine for fuel, oil, coolant and other leaks; determine necessary action (P-1)

Name _____ Date _____ Time on Task _____

Make/Model/Year _____ VIN _____ Evaluation: 4 3 2 1

_____ 1. The coolant level in the coolant recovery (surge) container should be at the cold level mark if cold or at the hot level if the coolant is hot.

     ____ **OK**

     ____ **NOT OK** (describe) _____

_____ 2. When the engine is cool, remove the radiator cap and check the coolant level.

     ____ **OK** – filled to the top

     ____ **NOT OK** (describe) _____

_____ 3. Visually check for coolant leaks.

     ____ **OK**

     ____ **NOT OK** (describe the location of the leak) _____

     _____

_____ 4. Pressure test the cooling system and check for a drop in pressure, which indicates a leak in the system.

     ____ **OK**

     ____ **NOT OK** (describe results)

_____

_____ 5. Based on the inspection and pressure test, what is the necessary action? _____

_____

_____

91

Intake System Smoke Test

Meets NATEF Task: (A1-A-5) Inspect engine for leaks; determine necessary action (P-1)

___

Name _____ Date _____ Time on Task _____

Make/Model/Year _____ VIN _____ Evaluation: 4   3   2   1

_____ **1.** Set up the intake system for smoke testing by removing the air inlet from the throttle body and cover by using one of the following (select one).

     _____ Plastic sheet held on by tape or rubber bands

     _____ Rubber (vinyl) glove covering the air inlet

     _____ Cardboard and tape

     _____ Other (describe)

_____

_____ **2.** Start the smoke machine and allow it to reach operating temperature.

_____ **3.** Disconnect the large vacuum hose from the vacuum brake booster. Attach the smoke machine to the hose (not to the vacuum booster).

_____ **4.** Inject smoke into the intake of the engine following the instructions for the smoke machine. Observe hoses and gasket areas for smoke.

     _____ No smoke visible

     _____ If smoke is visible, describe the location _____

_____ **5.** What is the necessary action? _____

_____ **6.** Disconnect the smoke machine and reattach the vacuum host to the vacuum brake booster. Check for proper engine operation.

92

Engine Noise and Vibration Diagnosis

Meets NATEF Task: (A1-A-6) Diagnose engine noises and vibration; determine necessary action (P-2)

Name _____ Date _____ Time on Task _____

Make/Model/Year _____ VIN _____ Evaluation: 4 3 2 1

_____ **1.** When is the engine noise or vibration detected? Check all that apply.

_____ At engine start (warm engine)

_____ At engine start (cold engine)

_____ Idle (cold)

_____ Idle (hot)

_____ During acceleration

_____ Under heavy load

_____ Under light load

_____ During deceleration

_____ Other (describe) _____

_____ **2.** Describe the noise or vibration. Check all that apply.

_____ Clicking sound (like a ball-point pen)

_____ Clacking noise (like tapping on metal)

_____ Rattle (like a baby rattle)

_____ Clatter (like rolling marbles)

_____ Whine (like an electric motor running)

_____ Clunk (like a door closing)

_____ Other (describe) _____

_____ **3.** Check service information regarding the noise and the associated tests and procedures that should be followed. _____

_____

_____ **4.** What is the necessary action? _____

_____

93

We Support
NATEF

Engine Exhaust and Sound Diagnosis

Meets NATEF Task: (A1-A-6) Diagnose engine noises and vibrations; determine necessary action. (P-2)

Name _____ Date _____ Time on Task _____

Make/Model/Year _____ VIN _____ Evaluation: 4 3 2 1

_____ **1.** Start the engine and observe the exhaust.

        _____ OK (no visible exhaust smoke)
        _____ Light amount of visible steam (usually normal)
        _____ Heavy white steam or smoke (possible coolant leak into the combustion chamber)
        _____ Black exhaust smoke (usually caused by a rich air-fuel mixture)
        _____ Gray exhaust for a second or two, then no exhaust smoke (normal)
        _____ Blue exhaust smoke at start-up, then normal exhaust (usually caused by defective valve stem seals)
        _____ Blue exhaust smoke all the time (engine is using oil)
        _____ Other (describe) _____

_____ **2.** Exhaust odor (exhaust does have some smell due to the various hydrocarbons used in the fuel).

        _____ Normal
        _____ Abnormal (if abnormal describe)

        _____

_____ **3.** Exhaust sound

        _____ Normal
        _____ Hissing (check for exhaust leak) and describe the location _____
        _____ Loud (determine the reason and the necessary action to correct the fault ___

        _____
        _____ Other (describe) _____

_____ **4.** Based on the analysis above, check service information to determine the steps needed to correct the concerns. _____

        _____

_____ **5.** What is the necessary action? _____

        _____

94

Exhaust System Smoke Test

Meets NATEF Task: (A1-A-7) Diagnose engine noises and vibrations; determine necessary action. (P-2)

Name _____ Date _____ Time on Task _____

Make/Model/Year _____ VIN _____ Evaluation: 4 3 2 1

_____ 1. Start the smoke machine and allow it to reach operating temperature.

_____ 2. Hoist the vehicle to be able to see the exhaust system.

_____ 3. Insert the discharge hose from the smoke machine into the tailpipe and start the flow of smoke.

_____ 4. Check for evidence of smoke from parts of the exhaust system, which indicates a leak.

       _____ No smoke visible

       _____ Smoke visible (describe the location)
       _____

_____ 5. Lower the vehicle and repeat the injection of smoke into the exhaust system.

_____ 6. Check for evidence of smoke from under the hood and around the intake manifold and exhaust gas recirculation (EGR) valve and piping.

       _____ No smoke visible

       _____ Smoke visible (describe the location) _____

_____ 7. What is the necessary action? _____

_____

_____ 8. Disconnect the smoke machine.

95

Vacuum Testing

Meets NATEF Task: (A1-A-8) Perform engine vacuum tests; determine necessary action (P-1)

Name _____ Date _____ Time on Task _____

Make/Model/Year _____ VIN _____ Evaluation: 4   3   2   1

_____ **1.** Connect the vacuum gauge to a manifold vacuum source (source of vacuum at idle).

_____ **2.** Vacuum at idle = _____ in. Hg. (should be 17-21 in. Hg. and steady).

_____ **3.** Drive the vehicle on a level road in high gear at a steady speed.

   Cruise vacuum = _____ in. Hg.   (should be 10 - 15 in. Hg.)

_____ **4.** Accelerate the vehicle in high gear to W.O.T.

   W.O.T. vacuum = _____ in. Hg.   (should be almost zero)

_____ **5.** Decelerate the vehicle from 50 MPH with the throttle closed.

   Deceleration vacuum = _____ in. Hg.   (should be higher than idle vacuum)

_____ **6.** With the engine out of gear and the brake firmly applied, raise the engine speed to 2,000 RPM and hold for one full minute. This tests for an exhaust restriction.

   Results = _____ in. Hg.

_____ **7.** Stop the engine. Disable the ignition. Crank the engine and observe the vacuum during cranking.

   Cranking vacuum = _____ in. Hg.   (should be higher than 2.5 in. Hg.)

   OK_____   **NOT OK**_____

_____ **8.** Based on the vacuum test results, what is the necessary action? _____

   _____

96

Paper Test

Meets NATEF Task: (A1-A-9) Perform cylinder power balance tests; determine necessary action (P-1)

Name _____ Date _____ Time on Task _____

Make/Model/Year _____ VIN _____ Evaluation: 4 3 2 1

_____ 1. The engine should be at normal operating temperature (the upper radiator hose hot and pressurized or the cooling fans cycled on and off).

_____ 2. Check the exhaust system for leaks (test results may not be valid if the exhaust system is not okay).

_____ 3. Start the engine and allow it to idle. A sound running engine should produce even and steady exhaust "puffs" at the tailpipe.

_____ 4. Hold a piece of paper (even a dollar bill works) or a 3" x 5" card within 1 inch (25 mm)
of the tailpipe with the engine running at idle. The paper should blow out evenly without "puffing."

      A. If the paper is drawn toward the tailpipe at times, the valves in one or more cylinders could be burned. Other possible problems if the paper is sucked toward the tailpipe include:

           1. The engine could be misfiring due to a lean condition that could occur normally when the engine is cold.

           2. Pulsing of the paper toward the tailpipe could also be caused by a hole in the exhaust system. If exhaust escapes through a hole in the exhaust system, air could be drawn from the tailpipe to the hole in the exhaust between the exhaust "puffs," causing the paper to be drawn toward the tailpipe.

      B. If the paper is unevenly pulsing outward, an engine misfire is a possibility. The usual cause of this is an ignition or an engine mechanical problem such as a worn camshaft or broken rocker arm.

_____ 5. Describe the results _____

_____

OK _____   NOT OK _____

97

Cylinder Power Balance Tests

Meets NATEF Task: (A1-A-9) Perform cylinder power balance tests; determine necessary action. (P-2)

Name _____ Date _____ Time on Task _____

Make/Model/Year _____ VIN _____ Evaluation: 4 3 2 1

_____ 1. An automotive diagnostic scope or digital storage oscilloscope with relative compression can be used to determine cylinder balance. Check all that apply.

      _____ Automotive diagnostic scope
      _____ Digital storage oscilloscope with relative compression capability
      _____ Other (describe) _____

_____ 2. Follow the equipment manufacturers' instructions and connect the tester to the engine. Instructions to connect to the engine include: _____
_____

_____ 3. Start the engine and allow it to reach normal operating temperature.

_____ 4. Follow the instructions of the test equipment manufacturer and perform a cylinder power balance test. Record the results.

      Cylinder #1 = _____   Cylinder #5 = _____
      Cylinder #2 = _____   Cylinder #6 = _____
      Cylinder #3 = _____   Cylinder #7 = _____
      Cylinder #4 = _____   Cylinder #8 = _____

_____ 5. If performing an engine speed (RPM) drop test, all cylinders should be within 50 RPM.

      _____ **OK**
      _____ **NOT OK** (describe results) _____
      _____ **NA**

_____ 6. If relative compression is being performed, all cylinders should be within 10%.

      _____ **OK**
      _____ **NOT OK** (describe results) _____
      _____ **NA**

98

Compression Testing

Meets NATEF Task: (A1-A-10) Perform cylinder compression tests; determine necessary action (P-1)

Name _____ Date _____ Time on Task _____

Make/Model/Year _____ VIN _____ Evaluation: 4 3 2 1

_____ **1.** Remove all spark plugs (be certain to label the spark plug wires) and disable the ignition system to avoid possible ignition coil damage.

_____ **2.** Block open the throttle and choke (if equipped).

_____ **3.** Crank the engine at least 4 "puffs" (compression strokes) while observing the gauge.

> **NOTE:** For accurate test results, the engine should be at normal operating temperature.
>
> **RESULTS: 1st puff / final reading**   **1st puff / final reading**
>
> 1. _____ / _____   5. _____ / _____
> 2. _____ / _____   6. _____ / _____
> 3. _____ / _____   7. _____ / _____
> 4. _____ / _____   8. _____ / _____
>
> **NOTE:** The 1st "puff" should be more than one-half of the pressure of the final puff. If the 1st puff is low, worn piston rings are likely – repeat the test.

_____ **4.** Reinstall all spark plugs except one. Perform a running compression test at idle and at 2000 RPM for each cylinder:

	Idle	2000 RPM
1.	_____	_____
2.	_____	_____
3.	_____	_____
4.	_____	_____
5.	_____	_____
6.	_____	_____
7.	_____	_____
8.	_____	_____

OK_____   NOT OK_____

_____ **5.** Based on the test results, what is the necessary action? _____

_____

99

Head Gasket Diagnosis

Meets NATEF Task: (A1-A-11) Perform cylinder leakage tests; determine necessary action.
(P-1)

Name _____ **Date** _____ **Time on Task** _____

Make/Model/Year _____ **VIN** _____ **Evaluation:** 4   3   2   1

A blown (defective) head gasket is often difficult to diagnose. To verify that a head gasket is defective, perform the following tests and checks.

_____ 1. Is excessive white steam visual at the tail pipe (disregard normal steam that occurs in cold weather)?

   OK _____   **NOT OK** _____

_____ 2. Check for visual signs of coolant or oil leakage between the block and the cylinder head.

   OK _____   **NOT OK** _____

_____ 3. Is the level of coolant lower than normal? (Lower than normal coolant level can indicate a defective head gasket.)

   OK _____   **NOT OK** _____

_____ 4. Does the engine run correctly (a blown head gasket often causes the engine to miss)?

   OK _____   **NOT OK** _____

_____ 5. Remove the radiator cap after the engine has cooled and use an exhaust gas analysis kit to determine whether exhaust gases are present in the coolant. One common test involves drawing coolant into a container with blue liquid in it and if it changes color to a yellow/green, then exhaust gases are present in the coolant.

   OK _____   **NOT OK** _____

_____ 6. Start the engine and use a 4- or 5-gas analyzer to check for CO and/or HC emissions above the open radiator cap.

   OK _____   **NOT OK** _____

_____ 7. Based on the tests results, what is the necessary action? _____

   _____

100

Cylinder Leakage Test

Meets NATEF Task: (A1-A-11) Perform cylinder leakage tests; determine necessary action. (P-1)

Name _____ Date _____ Time on Task _____

Make/Model/Year _____ VIN _____ Evaluation: 4 3 2 1

_____ **1.** The engine should be at normal operating temperature.

_____ **2.** Rotate the engine until the piston of the cylinder being tested is at TDC on the compression stroke.

_____ **3.** Calibrate the cylinder leakage gauge.

_____ **4.** Install compressed air in the cylinder. Read the gauge.

   _____ % of leakage

   Check one:

   _____ **Good** - less than 10%

   _____ **Acceptable** - less than 20%

   _____ **Unacceptable** - higher than 20%

_____ **5.** Check the *source* of air leakage:

   _____ a. **radiator** - possible blown head gasket or cracked cylinder head.

   _____ b. **tail pipe** - defective exhaust valve(s).

   _____ c. **carburetor or air inlet** - defective intake valve(s).

   _____ d. **oil filler cap** - possible worn or defective piston rings.

_____ **6.** Based on the test results, what is the necessary action? _____

_____

101

Oil Pressure Measurement

Meets NATEF Task: (A1-D-1) Perform oil pressure test; determine necessary action. (P-1)

Name _____ Date _____ Time on Task _____

Make/Model/Year _____ VIN _____ Evaluation: 4 3 2 1

_____ **1.** Locate the oil pressure-sending (sender) unit.

_____ **2.** Remove the sending unit using the proper size sending unit socket or wrench.

_____ **3.** Thread a mechanical oil pressure gauge into the thread portion of the engine block where the sending unit was located.

_____ **4.** Route the oil pressure gauge hose away from the moving components of the engine.

_____ **5.** Start the engine and check for leaks.

_____ **6.** Record the oil pressure:

        oil pressure @ idle _____

        oil pressure @ 1,000 RPM _____

        oil pressure @ 2,000 RPM _____

        oil pressure @ 3,000 RPM _____

        NOTE: Most engines require about 10 psi per 1,000 RPM.

Oil pressure gauge

Oil pressure sending unit hole

_____ **7.** Results: (check one)

        great _____ (over 10 psi per 1,000 RPM)

        good _____ (at 10 psi per 1,000 RPM)

        bad _____ (less than 10 psi per 1,000 RPM)

_____ **8.** Based on the test results, what is the necessary action? _____

_____

102

Water Pump Replacement

Meets NATEF Task: (A1-D-8) Inspect, remove and replace water pump. (P-2)

Name _____ Date _____ Time on Task _____

Make/Model/Year _____ VIN _____ Evaluation: 4 3 2 1

The water pump should be replaced if there is a coolant leak at the weep (vent) hole or pump gasket surface, or whenever a timing belt is replaced. The water pump can also be the cause of a lack of heat from the heater, because a pump that has eroded fins or has an impeller that is slipping on the shaft will not be able to circulate heated coolant through the long heater hose.

_____ 1. Check service information for the specified water pump inspection and testing plus replacement procedure. _____

_____

> *NOTE:* Drain the cooling system coolant into a suitable container and dispose of it properly, or recycle it.

_____ 2. Remove other components and brackets necessary to remove the water pump from the engine. The parts that needed to be removed included:

_____   _____

_____   _____

_____   _____

_____ 3. Clean the gasket surfaces.

_____ 4. Attach a new gasket to the water pump and install the pump.

_____ 5. Torque the retaining bolts to factory specifications.

Water pump retaining bolts torque specification = _____

_____ 6. Reinstall all components, brackets, hoses, and belts that were removed to access the water pump.

_____ 7. Refill the cooling system with new antifreeze coolant.

> **CAUTION:** Be sure to open the cooling system bleeder valves(s), if equipped, to avoid trapping air.

_____ 8. Install the radiator pressure cap and start the engine. Check for leaks and proper cooling system operation.

103

Timing Belt/Chain Replacement

Meets NATEF Task: (A1-B-11) Inspect and replace camshaft and drive belt/chain. (P-1)

Name _____ **Date** _____ **Time on Task** _____

Make/Model/Year _____ **VIN** _____ **Evaluation:** 4 3 2 1

_____ **1.** Check service information for the exact timing belt replacement procedure as specified by the vehicle manufacturer, including torque specifications.

_____

_____

_____

_____ **2.** Inspect the timing belt for wear or faults.

_____ **3.** List the parts recommended to be replaced when replacing the timing belt. (Usually includes the water pump, camshaft seals, crankshaft seals, and often the tensioner[s].)

SURFACE CRACK   WORN EDGE

SIDEWALL CRACK   PLY SEPARATION

_____

_____

_____ **4.** Describe the proper camshaft timing procedure. _____

_____

_____ **5.** What parts were inspected for wear? _____

_____

_____ **6.** What parts were replaced? _____

_____

104

Remove and Reinstall Engine (FWD)

Meets NATEF Task: (A1-A-12) Remove and reinstall engine in an OBD II or newer vehicle; reconnect all attaching components and restore the vehicle to running condition. (P-2)

Name _____ **Date** _____ **Time on Task** _____

Make/Model/Year _____ **VIN** _____ **Evaluation: 4   3   2   1**

_____ **1.** Check service information for the specified procedures to follow to remove and reinstall the engine in a front-wheel-drive vehicle. List the steps specified to remove the engine.

_____

_____

_____

_____

_____ **2.** Using service information, list the steps specified to reinstall the engine.

_____

_____

_____

_____

_____ **3.** List the parts or supplies needed to complete this task.

_____

_____

_____

105

Remove and Reinstall Engine (RWD)

Meets NATEF Task: (A1-A-12) Remove and reinstall engine in an OBD II or newer vehicle; reconnect all attaching components and restore the vehicle to running condition. (P-2)

Name _____ Date _____ Time on Task _____

Make/Model/Year _____ VIN _____ Evaluation: 4 3 2 1

_____ **1.** Check service information for the specified procedures to follow to remove and reinstall the engine in a rear-wheel-drive vehicle. List the steps specified to remove the engine.

_____

_____

_____

_____

_____ **2.** Using service information, list the steps specified to reinstall the engine.

_____

_____

_____

_____

_____ **3.** List the parts or supplies needed to complete this task.

_____

_____

_____

_____

106

We Support
NATEF

Engine Mount Replacement

Meets NATEF Task: (A1-A-15) Inspect, remove, and replace engine mounts.
(P-2)

Name _____ Date _____ Time on Task _____

Make/Model/Year _____ VIN _____ Evaluation: 4 3 2 1

_____ **1.** Check service information for the specified procedures to follow when replacing the

engine mounts. Describe the specified procedures. _____

_____

_____

_____ **2.** Based on the recommended test and inspection procedures, which engine mounts

require replacement? Describe the location. _____

_____

_____

_____ **3.** Describe the recommended
tools needed and the
procedures specified in
service information for
replacing the engine mounts.

_____

_____

_____

107

Remove Cylinder Head(s) and Inspect

Meets NATEF Task: (A1-B-1) Remove cylinder head; inspect gasket condition; install cylinder head, gasket; tighten according to manufacturer's specifications and procedures. (P-1)

Name _____ **Date** _____ **Time on Task** _____

Make/Model/Year _____ **VIN** _____ **Evaluation:** 4 3 2 1

_____ **1.** Check service information for the specified head bolt removal sequence.

> ***NOTE:*** Most vehicle manufacturers specify that the removal procedure should be the opposite of the tightening sequence to help avoid causing warpage of the cylinder head during removal.

Specified sequence: _____

_____ **2.** Visually check for cracks.

_____ **OK** _____ **NOT OK** (describe the fault) _____

_____ **3.** Check gasket surfaces for signs of leakage.

_____ **OK** _____ **NOT OK** (describe the fault) _____

_____ **4.** Clean the cylinder head.

_____ **5.** Using a machined straight edge and feeler gauges, check the fire deck surface of the cylinder head for warpage and compare to the specified maximum allowable variation in flatness.

Specified maximum cylinder head out-of-flatness = _____

Measured amount of warpage = _____ _____ **OK** _____ **NOT OK**

_____ **6.** Check oil, coolant, intake and exhaust passages for damage.

_____ **OK** _____ **NOT OK**

108

Engine Disassembly

Meets NATEF Task: (A1-C-1) Disassemble engine block; clean and prepare components for inspection and reassembly. (P-1)

Name _____ Date _____ Time on Task _____

Make/Model/Year _____ VIN _____ Evaluation: 4 3 2 1

This procedure is for overhead valve engines only. For overhead camshaft engines, consult the factory service information.

_____ 1. Remove all coolant and engine oil from the engine.

_____ 2. Clean the engine with degreaser and/or a pressure washer.

_____ 3. Install the engine on an engine stand.

_____ 4. Remove the exhaust and the intake manifolds.

_____ 5. Remove the cylinder head(s) being certain to follow the torque table backwards starting with the highest number and working toward the lowest number to help prevent warping the cylinder head.

_____ 6. Remove the harmonic balancer and timing chain cover.

_____ 7. Remove the timing chain and camshaft.

_____ 8. Remove the oil pan (replace all pan bolts back into the block rails to prevent loss if possible).

_____ 9. Remove the oil pickup and pump (if in the oil pan).

_____ 10. Mark the connecting rods if not already marked from the factory or during a previous service.

_____ 11. Remove the ridge:

    a. Install the tool into the cylinder and position the piston properly so that enough threads will be above the tool to cut the entire ridge.
    b. Expand the tool to the proper bore size.
    c. Locate the cutter blade slightly below the ridge and tighten the lock screw.
    d. Apply the spring tension to the cutter blade.
    e. Cut the ridge.
    f. Stop cutting as soon as the ridge has been removed to avoid tapering the top of the bore.
    g. Remove the chips from the cylinder.

_____ 12. Remove the pistons and the rods (keep the rod caps together).

109

Engine Block Disassembly

Meets NATEF Task: (A1-C-1) Disassemble engine block; clean and prepare components for inspection and reassembly. (P-2)

Name _____ Date _____ Time on Task _____

Make/Model/Year _____ VIN _____ Evaluation: 4 3 2 1

_____ 1. Check service information for the specified engine block disassembly procedures and precautions.

_____

_____

_____

_____ 2. Remove the pistons and connecting rod assemblies. Was it necessary to ream the ridge?   **Yes** _____   **No** _____

_____ 3. Remove the crankshaft.

_____ 4. Remove the camshafts (if applicable) and auxiliary and/or balance shafts.

_____ 5. Remove all expansion plugs.

_____ 6. Clean the engine block and all other parts. Describe the method(s) used to clean the block and parts.

_____

_____

_____

_____

110

Cylinder Wall Inspection

Meets NATEF Task: (A1-C-3) Inspect and measure cylinder walls; determine necessary action. (P-2)

Name _____ **Date** _____ **Time on Task** _____

Make/Model/Year _____ **VIN** _____ **Evaluation:** 4   3   2   1

_____ **1.** Check service information and determine the specified tests and inspection needed to be performed to determine the usable condition of the cylinder walls. What is the specified measurement and condition?

_____

_____

_____ **2.** What is the actual measurement and the specified measurement? _____

	Actual		**Actual**
Cylinder #1	_____	Cylinder #5	_____
Cylinder #2	_____	Cylinder #6	_____
Cylinder #3	_____	Cylinder #7	_____
Cylinder #4	_____	Cylinder #8	_____

_____ **3.** Based on the inspection and measurement, what is the necessary action? _____

_____

_____

_____

111

Cylinder Ridge Reaming

Meets NATEF Task: Not specified by NATEF

Name _____ **Date** _____ **Time on Task** _____

Make/Model/Year _____ **VIN** _____ **Evaluation:** 4   3   2   1

A ridge appears at the top of the cylinder where the piston rings do not travel. The ridge is actually the original size of the cylinder, and the area below the ridge is where the piston rings have worn the cylinder. Before removing the pistons, this ridge should be removed to help prevent damage to the pistons when they are pushed out of the top of the engine.

_____ **1.** Remove the cylinder head(s) from the engine.

_____ **2.** Rotate the crankshaft so that the piston is at the bottom of the cylinder before removing the ridge.

> Estimated thickness of the ridge = _____

_____ **3.** Install the ridge reamer and adjust the size of the cylinder with the cutter blade just below the ridge.

_____ **4.** Rotate the ridge reamer clockwise to remove the ridge.

_____ **5.** Repeat for the other cylinders.

112

Cleaning and Crack Detection

Meets NATEF Task: (A1-B-2) Inspect for cracks in cylinder head. (P-2)
Meets NATEF Task: (A1-C-2) Check for cracks in engine block. (P-2)

Name _____ Date _____ Time on Task _____

Make/Model/Year _____ VIN _____ Evaluation: 4 3 2 1

_____ 1. Double-check that all components, bolts, and plugs have been removed from the cylinder(s) and block.

_____ 2. Method used to clean the cylinder head(s) and/or block (check all that apply):

> **CAUTION:** Do not use steel or metal tools or scrapers on aluminum parts. Use only wooden or plastic scrapers.

_____ solvent-based cleaning   _____ hot tank chemical cleaning
_____ water-based chemical cleaning   _____ vapor cleaning
_____ spray washing   _____ ultrasonic cleaning
_____ steam cleaning   _____ vibratory cleaning
_____ thermal oven cleaning   _____ blasting with shot
_____ cold tank chemical cleaning

_____ 3. Visual inspection for faults. _____ **OK** _____ **NOT OK** (describe) _____

_____ 4. Check the cylinder head(s) and block for cracks. Which method(s) was used?

_____ magnetic (Magnafluxing®)
_____ dye penetrant (red dye and white powder)
_____ fluorescent penetrant (Zyglo®)
_____ pressure testing

_____ **OK** _____ **NOT OK** (describe) _____

_____ 5. If cracks were detected, what was the solution?

_____ replace the head/block
_____ stop drilling
_____ welding
_____ crack plugging
_____ other (describe) _____

Block Thread Inspection and Correction

Meets NATEF Task: (A1-C-3) Inspect Internal and External Threads; Restore as Needed. (P2)

Name _____ Date _____ Time on Task _____

Make/Model/Year _____ VIN _____ Evaluation: 4 3 2 1

_____ **1.** Check service information and determine the specified thread inspection methods and repair techniques.

_____

_____

_____

_____ **2.** Clean and inspect all engine bolts for thread damage, elongation, or damage.

OK _____ **NOT OK** _____ Describe faults: _____

_____

_____ **3.** Carefully clean all block internal threads using a thread chase or other recommended tool or procedure.

_____ **4.** Carefully inspect for damaged threads. **OK** _____ **NOT OK** _____

_____ **5.** Show the correct thread repair procedure as specified by the engine manufacturer.

Instructor's OK _____

114

Cylinder Head Specifications

Meets NATEF Task: (A1-A-3) Research applicable vehicle and service information, vehicle service history, service precautions, and technical service bulletins. (P-1)

Name _____ Date _____ Time on Task _____

Make/Model/Year _____ VIN _____ Evaluation: 4 3 2 1

_____ **1.** Type of material: _____ cast iron or _____ aluminum alloy

_____ **2.** What is the maximum allowable surface variation (out-of-flat)?

_____

_____ **3.** Valve seat runout (maximum): _____

_____ **4.** Intake valve seat angle: _____

_____ **5.** Intake valve face angle: _____

_____ **6.** Intake valve seat width: _____

_____ **7.** Exhaust valve seat angle: _____

_____ **8.** Exhaust valve face angle: _____

_____ **9.** Exhaust valve seat width: _____

_____ **10.** Type of valve guide:

  _____ integral (cast iron heads only)

  _____ powdered metal

  _____ other (specify) _____

_____ **11.** Valve guide bore diameter: _____

_____ **12.** Minimum valve margins: intake valve _____ exhaust valve _____

_____ **13.** Type of valve rotators:

  _____ positive on exhaust valve only

  _____ free type (keepers touching together)

  _____ not used on this engine

_____ **14.** Location of valve rotators:

  _____ above the valve spring

  _____ under the valve spring

  _____ not used on this engine

115

Cylinder Head Disassembly

Meets NATEF Task: (A1-B-1) Remove cylinder head(s); visually inspect for cracks; check gasket surface areas for leakage; check passage condition. (P-2)

Name _____ **Date** _____ **Time on Task** _____

Make/Model/Year _____ **VIN** _____ **Evaluation:** 4 3 2 1
Engine _____ **Displacement** _____

_____ 1. Remove the camshaft(s) if overhead camshaft design.

_____ 2. Remove the rocker arm/cam followers and place them in order so that the parts can be assembled in the same location.

> **NOTE:** All parts wear during operation and each part tends to wear slightly differently, so this is an important step that assures proper reassembly.

_____ 3. Remove the hydraulic lifter/lash adjuster, if equipped, and place them so that they can be reinstalled in the same location.

_____ 4. Use a dead blow (plastic shot-filled) hammer and tap the valve spring retainer to "break the taper" of the valve keepers (locks).

_____ 5. Use a valve spring compressor to compress the valves and remove the keepers. Remove the valve from the cylinder head and place the valve, spring, retainer, and keepers together for inspection and reassembly.

_____ 6. Are valve rotators used on this engine?

_____ Yes (If yes, where are they located?) _____
_____
_____ No

_____ 7. Remove the valve stem seals and spring seat (if aluminum head).

_____ 8. Type of valve stem seals?

_____ positive (over guide)
_____ umbrella (on valve stem)
_____ O-ring (in groove of valve)
_____ part of the valve spring seat

116

Cylinder Head Flatness Measurement

Meets NATEF Task: (A1-B-2) Clean and visually inspect a cylinder head for cracks; check gasket surface areas for warpage and surface finish; check passage condition. (P-1)

Name _____ Date _____ Time on Task _____

Make/Model/Year _____ VIN _____ Evaluation: 4 3 2 1

_____ **1.** What is the maximum allowable out-of-flatness according to factory specifications?

_____

_____ **2.** Thoroughly clean the fire deck surface of the cylinder head using the appropriate cleaning method:

- **cast iron cylinder heads**
    bristle discs:
    a. green (coarse – 50 grit)
    b. yellow (medium – 80 grit)
    scraper

- **aluminum cylinder heads**
    bristle discs:
    a. yellow (medium – 80 grit)
    b. white (fine – 120 grit)
    plastic or wooden scraper

_____ **3.** Use a precision straight edge and a feeler (thickness) gauge to check for warpage, distortion, bend and twist by checking in five places.

_____ **4.** Maximum thickness of feeler gauge that could be placed between the straight edge and the head is _____ inches.

OK _____   NOT OK _____

_____ **5.** What is the necessary action? _____

_____

117

Valve Spring Inspection

Meets NATEF Task: (A1-B-3) Inspect valve springs for squareness and free height; determine necessary action. (P-3)

Name _____ **Date** _____ **Time on Task** _____

Make/Model/Year _____ **VIN** _____ **Evaluation: 4   3   2   1**

_____ **1.** Check service information for the specified allowable tolerance when checking valve spring for squareness and free height. What is the specified tolerance?

           Squareness = _____

           Free height = _____

_____ **2.** Measure and inspect all springs:

		Squareness	Free height
Cylinder #1	Intake	_____	_____
	Exhaust	_____	_____
Cylinder #2	Intake	_____	_____
	Exhaust	_____	_____
Cylinder #3	Intake	_____	_____
	Exhaust	_____	_____
Cylinder #4	Intake	_____	_____
	Exhaust	_____	_____
Cylinder #5	Intake	_____	_____
	Exhaust	_____	_____
Cylinder #6	Intake	_____	_____
	Exhaust	_____	_____
Cylinder #7	Intake	_____	_____
	Exhaust	_____	_____
Cylinder #8	Intake	_____	_____
	Exhaust	_____	_____

_____ **3.** Based on the inspection and measurements, what is the necessary action?

_____

_____

_____

_____

118

Valve Guide Specifications and Measurement

Meets NATEF Task: (A1-B-5) Inspect valve guides for wear, check valve stem-to-guide clearance; determine necessary action. (P-3)

Name _____ **Date** _____ **Time on Task** _____

Make/Model/Year _____ **VIN** _____ **Evaluation:** 4 3 2 1

_____ 1. Specification for valve guide bore diameter: _____

_____ 2. Specification for maximum valve guide wear: _____

_____ 3. Use a small hole (split-ball) gauge and a 0-1" micrometer
to measure the valve guide at three locations.

        Top of the guide: _____

        Middle of the guide: _____

        Bottom of the guide: _____

        OK ____   **NOT OK** ____

_____ 4. If the valve guides are worn beyond factory limits, select the replacement type.

        _____ ream and install oversize (OS) valves

        _____ thin wall bronze

        _____ cast iron

        _____ powdered metal (PM)

        _____ other (describe): _____

_____ 5. What is the necessary action? _____

_____

119

Valve Guide Replacement

Meets NATEF Task: Not specified by NATEF

Name _____ Date _____ Time on Task _____

Make/Model/Year _____ VIN _____ Evaluation: 4   3   2   1

_____ **1.** Cylinder head material?

       _____ aluminum

       _____ cast iron

_____ **2.** Type of existing valve guides?

       _____ integral (cast-iron cylinder heads only)

       _____ cast iron

       _____ bronze

_____ **3.** Reason for valve replacement?

       _____ excessively worn (How much wear?) _____

       _____ damage (describe) _____

_____ **4.** Drill out old valve guides or drive out old guides.

       size of drill used = _____

_____ **5.** Ream the hole after drilling.

       Size of reamer used = _____

_____ **6.** Drive (or press) replacement guides into the cylinder head.

       type of replacement guide = _____

120

We Support
NATEF

Valve Guide Knurling

Meets NATEF Task: Not specified by NATEF

Name _____ **Date** _____ **Time on Task** _____

Make/Model/Year _____ **VIN** _____ **Evaluation:** 4 3 2 1

_____ **1.** Clean the valve guide with a guide cleaning tool.

_____ **2.** Lubricate the knurling tool.

_____ **3.** Knurl the valve guide by slowly running the tool through the guide.

_____ **4.** Ream the guide to the original nominal size with the special reamer.

   Size of reamer used = _____

_____ **5.** Clean the knurled valve guide carefully.

_____ **6.** Check for proper valve guide clearance.

   OK _____   **NOT OK** _____

121

Aluminum Cylinder Head Straightening

Meets NATEF Task: M1 Machinist task not specified by NATEF

Name _____ Date _____ Time on Task _____

Make/Model/Year _____ VIN _____ Evaluation: 4 3 2 1

Check service information and determine the following information.

_____ **1.** Specifications for out-of-flatness: _____

_____ **2.** Measured actual out-of-flatness: _____

_____ **3.** Before machining the surface of the cylinder head, place the head onto a flat 2" thick steel plate.

_____ **4.** Place shims equal to one-half of the warpage (out-of-flatness) of the head under both ends of the cylinder head.

       thickness of shims used: _____

_____ **5.** Bolt the center of the head to the plate using head bolts.

_____ **6.** Place the cylinder head into a 500° F oven and heat for at least 8 hours.

NOTE: The heat from the oven not only straightens the cylinder head, but it also stress relieves the head.

_____ **7.** Turn off the oven, and allow the cylinder head to cool gradually (at least 8 hours).

_____ **8.** After allowing the cylinder head to cool, measure the out-of-flatness: _____

_____ **9.** Machine the cylinder head as necessary.

122

Cylinder Head Assembly Inspection

Meets NATEF Task: (A1-B-2) Identify and interpret engine concern; determine necessary action. (P-3)

Name _____ Date _____ Time on Task _____

Make/Model/Year _____ VIN _____ Evaluation: 4 3 2 1

_____ 1. Oil the valve stem and install the valve in the head.

_____ 2. Install the retainer or rotator on the stem along with the locks (keeper) and pull them up tight.

_____ 3. Measure the installed height from the spring seat to the underside of the retainer or rotator.

Check service information and determine installed height specification _____
Record the actual installed height for each valve:
Left head intakes _____ _____ _____ _____
Left head exhaust _____ _____ _____ _____
Right head intakes _____ _____ _____ _____

Right head exhaust _____ _____ _____ _____

_____ 4. Record the thickness of the inserts (shims) required to restore the correct installed height (necessary action):

Left head intakes _____ _____ _____ _____
Left head exhaust _____ _____ _____ _____
Right head intakes _____ _____ _____ _____
Right head exhaust _____ _____ _____ _____

SPRING RETAINER

INSTALLED HEIGHT

STEM HEIGHT

SPRING SEAT

_____ 5. Check service information and determine the specified valve stem height. _____

_____ 6. Record the valve stem height.

Left head intakes _____ _____ _____ _____
Left head exhaust _____ _____ _____ _____
Right head intakes _____ _____ _____ _____
Right head exhaust _____ _____ _____ _____

_____ 7. What is the necessary action? _____

123

Valve Spring Specifications & Measurements

Meets NATEF Task: (A1-B-3) Inspect Valve Springs for Squareness and Free Height Comparison; Determine Necessary Action (P-3)

Name _____ Date _____ Time on Task _____

Make/Model/Year _____ VIN _____ Evaluation: 4 3 2 1

Engine _____ VIN _____

Check service information and determine the following:

_____ 1. Are the intake and exhaust valve springs interchangeable?

    (Some have different spring tension and some springs are wound in the opposite

    direction)   **Yes** _____   **No** _____

_____ 2. Check squareness (should be within 1/16"): _____ **OK** ____ **NOT OK** ____

_____ 3. The free length (height) specification: _____

_____ 4. The actual free length (height) (one intake and one exhaust spring):

    _____ intake spring   _____ exhaust spring

    OK _____   **NOT OK** _____

_____ 5. Valve closed load specification: _____ at _____ in. height.

_____ 6. Measured valve spring closed load:

    _____ intake spring   _____ exhaust spring

    OK _____   **NOT OK** _____

_____ 7. Valve open load specification: _____ at _____ in. height.

_____ 8. Measured valve spring closed load:

    _____ intake valve   _____ exhaust valve **OK** _____ **NOT OK** _____

_____ 9. Installed height specification: _____

_____ 10. Measured installed height: _____ intake valve _____ exhaust valve

    OK _____   **NOT OK** _____

_____ 11. Valve stem height specification: _____ in.

_____ 12. Measured valve stem height:

    _____ intake valve   _____ exhaust valve

    OK _____   **NOT OK** _____

124

Valve Spring Squareness and Free Height

Meets NATEF Task: (A1-B-3) Inspect Valve Spring for Squareness and Free Height Comparison; Determine Necessary Action. (P-2)

Name _____ **Date** _____ **Time on Task** _____

Make/Model/Year _____ **VIN** _____ **Evaluation: 4   3   2   1**

_____ **1.** Check service information and determine:

Spring free height = _____
Squareness = _____ (usually within 1/16 in. [1.6 mm])

_____ **2.** Measure the valve spring **free height** and **squareness**.

Cylinder #1	Intake	_____/_____	OK ____	NOT OK ____
	Exhaust	_____/_____	OK ____	NOT OK ____
Cylinder #2	Intake	_____/_____	OK ____	NOT OK ____
	Exhaust	_____/_____	OK ____	NOT OK ____
Cylinder #3	Intake	_____/_____	OK ____	NOT OK ____
	Exhaust	_____/_____	OK ____	NOT OK ____
Cylinder #4	Intake	_____/_____	OK ____	NOT OK ____
	Exhaust	_____/_____	OK ____	NOT OK ____
Cylinder #5	Intake	_____/_____	OK ____	NOT OK ____
	Exhaust	_____/_____	OK ____	NOT OK ____
Cylinder #6	Intake	_____/_____	OK ____	NOT OK ____
	Exhaust	_____/_____	OK ____	NOT OK ____
Cylinder #7	Intake	_____/_____	OK ____	NOT OK ____
	Exhaust	_____/_____	OK ____	NOT OK ____
Cylinder #8	Intake	_____/_____	OK ____	NOT OK ____
	Exhaust	_____/_____	OK ____	NOT OK ____

_____ **3.** Based on the results, what is the necessary action? _____

_____

125

Valve Stem Seal Replacement

Meets NATEF Task: (A1-B-4) Replace valve stem seals; inspect components; determine necessary action. (P-3)

Name _____ Date _____ Time on Task _____

Make/Model/Year _____ VIN _____ Evaluation: **4 3 2 1**

_____ **1.** Check service information for the specified tool(s) and procedures to follow to replace the valve stem seals on an assembled engine. Describe the specified procedures.

_____

_____

SEAL

TOOL

_____ **2.** What tools were specified to be used? _____

_____

_____ **3.** Based on the inspection of the valve spring retainers and locks, what is the necessary action? _____

_____

_____

126

Valve and Seat Inspection

Meets NATEF Task: (A1-B-6) Inspect Valves and Valve Seats; Determine Necessary Action.
(P-3)

Name _____ Date _____ Time on Task _____

Make/Model/Year _____ VIN _____ Evaluation: 4 3 2 1

_____ **1.** Check service information to determine the specified procedures to follow and the specification for valves and valve seats.

_____ **2.** Valves procedure: _____

_____

_____ **3.** Valves specifications: _____

_____

_____ **4.** Valve measurement: **OK** _____   **NOT OK** _____

If not OK, what is the necessary action?

_____

_____ **5.** Valve seat procedure: _____

_____

_____ **6.** Valve seat specifications: _____

_____

_____ **7.** Valve seat measurement: _____

OK _____   **NOT OK** _____   If not OK, what is the necessary action?

_____

_____

127

Valve Seat Inspection and Measurement

Meets NATEF Task: (A1-B-7) Check Valve Face-to-Seat Contact and Valve Seat Concentricity (Runout); Determine Necessary Action. (P-3)

Name _____ Date _____ Time on Task _____

Make/Model/Year _____ VIN _____ Evaluation: 4 3 2 1

_____ 1. Check service information for the specified procedure to determine the condition of the valve face-to-seat contact.

_____

_____

_____ 2. Inspect the valve face-to-seat contact and determine if it meets the specified standards.

OK _____ **NOT OK** _____ If not OK, state the reasons.

_____

_____

_____ 3. Check service information to determine the specified procedure to follow and the specifications for valve seat runout.

a. Specified procedure (list tools needed):_____

_____

b. Specifications for valve seat runout: _____

_____

_____ 4. Using the specified procedure, determine the valve seat runout = _____

OK _____ **NOT OK** _____ If not OK, state the reasons.

_____

_____

128

Valve Spring Assembled Height

Meets NATEF Task: (A1-B-7) Check valve spring assembled height and valve stem height; determine necessary action. (P-3)

Name _____ Date _____ Time on Task _____

Make/Model/Year _____ VIN _____ Evaluation: 4 3 2 1

_____ **1.** Check service information for the specified assembled height and valve stem height.

    a. Specified assembled height = _____

    b. Specified valve stem height = _____

_____ **2.** Actual measured assembled and valve stem height:

	Assembled Height	Valve Stem Height
1	_____	_____
2	_____	_____
3	_____	_____
4	_____	_____
5	_____	_____
6	_____	_____
7	_____	_____
8	_____	_____
9	_____	_____
10	_____	_____
11	_____	_____
12	_____	_____
13	_____	_____
14	_____	_____
15	_____	_____
16	_____	_____

_____ **3.** Based on the measurements and the recommendations stated in service information, what is the necessary action?

_____

_____

_____

129

Valve Face Grinding

Meets NATEF Task: Not specified by NATEF

Name _____ Date _____ Time on Task _____

Make/Model/Year _____ VIN _____ Evaluation: 4 3 2 1

_____ 1. Set up the dressing tool and dress the wheel. Make sure the lubricant is running over the diamond; remove no more than one thousandth of an inch at a pass.

_____ 2. Remove the carbon and dirt from the valve.

_____ 3. Set the chuck fixture to the proper valve face angle.

_____ 4. Remove the valve stem and install the chamfer tool so the end almost touches the wheel.

_____ 5. Start the machine and slide the stem into the chamfer tool. While slowly rotating the valve, grind a slight chamfer on the stem.

_____ 6. Adjust the chuck to hold the valve tightly in the chuck about 1-2 in.

_____ 7. Start the machine and rotate the valve checking for a bent stem.

_____ 8. Start the machine and bring the valve face to the center of the grinding wheel.

_____ 9. Slowly turn the crossfeed knob to just touch the valve face. Adjust the lubricant to flow over the face.

_____ 10. Note and record the reading on the crossfeed shaft.

_____ 11. Grind the valve face, removing only as much material as necessary to get a smooth uniform finish. While grinding, move the valve back and forth across the face of the stone while turning the crossfeed.

_____ 12. Check the valve face for a good finish before removing it from the chuck.

_____ 13. Record the final reading on the crossfeed shaft and subtract the initial reading from it.

_____ 14. Insert the valve stem in the holder and zero the graduation ring and start the machine. Grind the valve stem **one-half the amount you ground off the face** in one thousandths increments.

130

Valve Seat Grinding

Meets NATEF Task: Not specified by NATEF

Name _____ Date _____ Time on Task _____

Make/Model/Year _____ VIN _____ Evaluation: 4 3 2 1

_____ 1. Clean the valve guide.

_____ 2. Choose the proper pilot for the guide.

_____ 3. Insert the pilot. (Do not force the pilot.)

_____ 4. Select the proper stones for each valve size. Make sure that the stones will not contact the side of the combustion chamber.

_____ 5. Dress the stones to the proper angles for grinding.

_____ 6. Grind the seat angle first. The width should be 1/8" to 3/16" wide.

   OK _____ NOT OK _____

_____ 7. Grind the topping angle.

_____ 8. Grind the throating angle.

_____ 9. When finished, the seat width should be 1/16" approximately.

   OK _____ NOT OK _____

SEAT GRINDING SPECIFICATIONS

Intake Valve

Seat angle _____   Throat angle _____
Topping angle _____   Interference angle _____
Seat width _____   Pilot size _____

Exhaust Valve

Seat angle _____   Throat angle _____
Topping angle _____   Interference angle _____
Seat width _____   Pilot size _____

Camshaft Specification

Meets NATEF Task: (A1-A-3) Research applicable vehicle and service information. (P-1)

Name _____ **Date** _____ **Time on Task** _____

Make/Model/Year _____ **VIN** _____ **Evaluation: 4 3 2 1**

Check service information and determine the following information.

_____ **1.** Intake valve opens @: _____

_____ **2.** Intake valve closes @: _____

_____ **3.** Intake valve duration: _____ degrees

_____ **4.** Exhaust valve opens @: _____

_____ **5.** Exhaust valve closes @: _____

_____ **6.** Exhaust valve duration: _____ degrees

_____ **7.** Valve overlap: _____ degrees

_____ **8.** Camshaft journal diameters: front_____, _____, _____, _____ rear

_____ **9.** Specification for camshaft bearing oil clearance: _____

TOP DEAD CENTER

INTAKE VALVE OPENS

EXHAUST VALVE CLOSES

27°

30°

DIRECTION OF ROTATION

264° REF.

INTAKE VALVE CLOSES

54°

67°

EXHAUST VALVE OPENS

BOTTOM DEAD CENTER

EXHAUST STROKE
INTAKE STROKE

132

Pushrods and Rocker Arm Inspection

Meets NATEF Task: (A1-B-8) Inspect pushrods and rocker arms; determine necessary action. (P-2)

Name _____ Date _____ Time on Task _____

Make/Model/Year _____ VIN _____ Evaluation: 4   3   2   1

_____ 1. Check service information for the specified procedures to follow when inspecting

pushrods and rocker arms. Describe the specified procedures: _____

_____

_____

_____

_____ 2. Based on the inspections, what is the necessary action? _____

_____

_____

_____

133

Valve Train Inspection

Meets NATEF Task: (A1-B-8) Inspect pushrods, rocker arms, rocker arm pivots and shafts for wear, bending, cracks, looseness, and blocked oil passages; determine necessary action. (P-2)

Name _____ Date _____ Time on Task _____

Make/Model/Year _____ VIN _____ Evaluation: 4 3 2 1

_____ **1.** Check service information and determine the specified procedures to follow when inspecting valve train components.

_____

_____

_____ **2.** Carefully inspect all of the pushrods for the following:

    a. Straightness by rolling on a flat surface   OK ____ NOT OK ____

    b. Rocker arms for wear or damage   OK ____ NOT OK ____

    c. Rocker arm pivots for wear or damage   OK ____ NOT OK ____

    d. Rocker arm shafts for wear or blocked oil passages   OK ____ NOT OK ____

_____ **3.** Describe all faults: _____

_____

_____

_____ **4.** What is the necessary action?

> **NOTE:** Some vehicle manufacturers recommend that the hollow pushrods not be reused. Because all of the dirt cannot be removed from the inside, it may dislodge and cause excessive wear if the pushrods are reused.

_____

_____

_____

134

Valve Lifter Inspection

Meets NATEF Task: (A1-B-9) Inspect valve lifters; determine necessary action.
(P-2)

Name _____ Date _____ Time on Task _____

Make/Model/Year _____ VIN _____ Evaluation: 4 3 2 1

_____ **1.** Check service information for the specified procedures and measurements when

inspecting valve lifters. Describe specified procedures and measurements.

_____

_____

_____

_____ **2.** Based on the specified inspection procedures, what is the necessary action? _____

_____

_____

_____

135

Valve Adjustment

Meets NATEF Task: (A1-B-10) Adjust valves (mechanical or hydraulic lifters).
(P1)

Name _____ Date _____ Time on Task _____

Make/Model/Year _____ VIN _____ Evaluation: 4 3 2 1

_____ **1.** Check service information and determine the specified procedure to follow to adjust the valves. List the procedure:

_____

_____

SPECIAL TOOL   ADJUSTING DISC   MAGNET

_____ **2.** Compare the original valve clearance or adjustment to the specified clearance.

		Original	Specified
Cylinder #1	Intake	_____	_____
	Exhaust	_____	_____
Cylinder #2	Intake	_____	_____
	Exhaust	_____	_____
Cylinder #3	Intake	_____	_____
	Exhaust	_____	_____
Cylinder #4	Intake	_____	_____
	Exhaust	_____	_____
Cylinder #5	Intake	_____	_____
	Exhaust	_____	_____
Cylinder #6	Intake	_____	_____
	Exhaust	_____	_____
Cylinder #7	Intake	_____	_____
	Exhaust	_____	_____
Cylinder #8	Intake	_____	_____
	Exhaust	_____	_____

136

Camshaft Inspection

Meets NATEF Task: (A1-B-12) Check camshaft for wear, damage, and out-of-round; determine necessary action. (P-2)

Name _____ **Date** _____ **Time on Task** _____

Make/Model/Year _____ **VIN** _____ **Evaluation: 4 3 2 1**

_____ **1.** Check service information for the specified inspection procedures and specifications.

　　　　a. List the inspection procedures: _____

　　　　_____

　　　　b. List camshaft specifications: _____

　　　　_____

_____ **2.** Measure the camshaft and compare with factory specifications.

　　　　____ **OK**　　　　____ **NOT OK** (describe the fault) _____

　　　　_____

_____ **3.** Based on the inspection and measurement of the camshaft, what is the necessary

　　　　action? _____

　　　　_____

　　　　_____

137

Timing Chain Diagnosis

Meets NATEF Task: (A1-B-12) Inspect and/or measure camshaft for runout, journal wear and lobe wear. (P-2)

Name _____ Date _____ Time on Task _____

Make/Model/Year _____ VIN _____ Evaluation: 4 3 2 1

A worn or stretched timing chain will cause the engine to produce lower than normal power at lower speeds but normal power at higher speeds.

_____ **1.** Disable the ignition system.

_____ **2.** Rotate the engine to TDC on the timing mark in normal direction of engine rotation (clockwise as viewed from the front of the engine).

_____ **3.** Remove the distributor cap (if equipped).

_____ **4.** Rotate the engine counterclockwise as viewed from the front of the engine until the rotor just starts to move.

> **NOTE:** On engines equipped with a distributorless ignition, observe the movement of the valve train through the oil fill hole rather than the distributor rotor.

_____ **5.** Record the number of degrees of slack in the timing chain.

_____ number of degrees of slack

OK _____   **NOT OK** _____

Results:

    1. less than 5° = normal.

    2. 5° - 8° = some change in engine operation if the timing chain is replaced.

    3. over 8° = new timing chain definitely required.

_____ **6.** What is the necessary action? _____

_____

138

Camshaft Bearing Surface Inspection

Meets NATEF Task: (A1-B-13) Inspect camshaft bearing surface for wear, damage, out-of-round, and alignment; determine necessary action. (P-2)

Name _____ Date _____ Time on Task _____

Make/Model/Year _____ VIN _____ Evaluation: 4 3 2 1

_____ **1.** Check service information for the specified procedures and measurements when inspecting a camshaft bearing surface. Describe specified procedures and specifications.

    a. Procedures: _____

    _____

    b. Camshaft bearing surface specifications: _____

    _____

_____ **2.** Based on the inspection and measurements, what is the necessary action?

_____

_____

_____

139

Camshaft Position Sensor

Meets NATEF Task: (A1-B-14) Establish camshaft position sensor indexing. (P-1)

Name _____ Date _____ Time on Task _____

Make/Model/Year _____ VIN _____ Evaluation: 4 3 2 1

_____ **1.** Check service information for the exact procedure to follow to index the camshaft

position sensor. Describe the procedure. _____

_____

_____

_____ **2.** Check all that apply about the specified procedures:

_____ Requires a scan tool

_____ Required if the timing chain/belt is replaced

_____ Requires special holding tools

_____ Other (describe) _____

_____

140

Connecting Rod Specification/Measurement

Meets NATEF Task: (A1-A-3) Research applicable vehicle and service information. (P-1)

Name _____ Date _____ Time on Task _____

Make/Model/Year _____ VIN _____ Evaluation: 4 3 2 1

_____ **1.** Type of connecting rod.

           _____ forged (wide parting line)

           _____ cast (narrow parting line)

           _____ powdered metal (smooth appearance)

_____ **2.** Is the rod equipped with an oil squirt hole near the big end to help lubricate the cylinder well and piston pin?

           Yes _____ **No** _____

_____ **3.** Type of piston pin.

           _____ press fit in the rod

           _____ full floating (uses piston pin retainers)

_____ **4.** Piston pin clearance specification: _____

_____ **5.** Measured piston pin clearance in the piston: _____

           OK _____ **NOT OK** _____

_____ **6.** Connecting rod big end diameter specification: _____

_____ **7.** Measure the connecting rod big end diameter: _____

           OK _____ **NOT OK** _____

PARTING
LINE

141

Piston and Bearing Wear Patterns

Meets NATEF Task: (A1-C-8) Identify piston and bearing wear patterns that connecting rod alignment and main bearing bore problems; determine necessary action. (P-3)

Name _____ **Date** _____ **Time on Task** _____

Make/Model/Year _____ **VIN** _____ **Evaluation: 4 3 2 1**

_____ 1. Check service information to determine procedures and specifications for connecting rod and main bearing bore alignment.

_____

_____

_____ 2. Visually inspect the piston skirts for *diagonal wear*, which could indicate a bent connecting rod.

OK ____   **NOT OK** ____

_____ 3. Visually inspect the connecting rod bearings for abnormal wear patterns.

OK ____   **NOT OK** ____   Describe faults: _____

_____

_____ 4. Visually inspect the main bearings for abnormal wear patterns.

OK ____   **NOT OK** ____   Describe faults: _____

_____

_____ 5. Using the specified procedure and equipment, check the connecting rods for proper alignment.

OK ____   **NOT OK** ____   Describe faults: _____

_____

_____ 6. Using the specified procedure and equipment, check the main bearing bore for proper alignment.

OK ____   **NOT OK** ____   Describe faults: _____

_____

142

Piston Pin Replacement

Meets NATEF Task: (A1-C-10) Remove and replace piston pin. (P-3)

Name _____ Date _____ Time on Task _____

Make/Model/Year _____ VIN _____ Evaluation: 4 3 2 1

_____ **1.** Check service information and determine the specified procedures and equipment needed to replace a piston pin.

_____

_____

_____ **2.** What type of piston pin retaining method is used?

_____ a. Interference fit

_____ b. Free-floating

SNAP RING

WRIST PIN

PISTON   MACHINED SLOT

143

Piston Ring Fitting

Meets NATEF Task: (A1-C-12) Inspect, measure and install piston rings. (P-1)

Name _____ Date _____ Time on Task _____

Make/Model/Year _____ VIN _____ Evaluation: 4 3 2 1

Piston rings should be fitted to each cylinder of the engine. The end gap of the rings is critical for best engine operation.

_____ **1.** Determine the following specifications for the engine being serviced:

        Ring end gap = _____ (usually 0.004" per inch of bore)

        Ring side clearance = _____ (usually 0.001" to 0.003")

_____ **2.** Select the top compressing ring and install it into the cylinder. Use a piston inserted upside down into the top of the bore to position the ring squarely in the cylinder.

_____ **3.** Use a feeler (thickness) gauge to measure the ring end gap:

        Ring end gap = _____

        OK _____   NOT OK _____

_____ **4.** If the gap is less than specified, use a file or ring file tool to increase the end gap until the specified gap is obtained.

_____ **5.** Repeat the procedure for the second compression ring.

_____ **6.** Repeat the procedure for all other rings and cylinders.

_____ **7.** Before installing the rings on the piston, be sure that there is the specified side clearance by inserting the piston ring backward into the piston ring groove and measuring the side clearance with a feeler gauge.

        Actual side clearance = _____

        OK _____   NOT OK _____

144

Piston Ring Specification and Measurement

Meets NATEF Task: (A1-C-12) Inspect, measure and install piston rings. (P-2)

Name _____ **Date** _____ **Time on Task** _____

Make/Model/Year _____ **VIN** _____ **Evaluation: 4   3   2   1**

_____ 1. Install each ring into the designated cylinder by inverting the piston and pushing each ring into the cylinder. Measure the piston ring gap (should be about 0.004 in. for each inch of bore).

	Specification	Actual	OK	NOT OK
Top ring	_____	_____	___	___
2nd compression ring	_____	_____	___	___
Oil control ring	_____	_____	___	___

_____ 2. File the butt ends of the rings as necessary to achieve proper ring gap.

_____ 3. Install the piston rings on the pistons.

_____ 4. Measure the piston ring side clearance: (usually about 0.001-0.003 in.)

	Specification	Actual	OK	NOT OK
Top ring	_____	_____	___	___
2nd compression ring	_____	_____	___	___
Oil control ring	_____	_____	___	___

_____ 5. Push on the face of all piston rings checking to make sure that they go fully into the ring groove, so that the ring face is flush or slightly recessed with the surface of the piston ring lands.

OK _____   **NOT OK** _____

145

Piston Inspection and Measurement

Meets NATEF Task: (A1-C-9) Inspect and measure piston skirts and ring leads; determine necessary action. (P-2)

Name _____ **Date** _____ **Time on Task** _____

Make/Model/Year _____ **VIN** _____ **Evaluation: 4   3   2   1**

_____ **1.** Check service information for the specified measurements and inspection procedures. State recommended procedures. _____

_____

_____

_____ **2.** What is the specified piston skirt size? Measure and record the piston skirt diameter.

Piston cylinder #1 = _____   Piston cylinder #5 = _____

Piston cylinder #2 = _____   Piston cylinder #6 = _____

Piston cylinder #3 = _____   Piston cylinder #7 = _____

Piston cylinder #4 = _____   Piston cylinder #8 = _____

_____ **3.** Based on the measurement and the inspection, what is the necessary action? _____

_____

_____

_____

146

Connecting Rod Reconditioning

Meets NATEF Task: (Not specified by NATEF)

Name _____ Date _____ Time on Task _____

Make/Model/Year _____ VIN _____ Evaluation: 4   3   2   1

_____ **1.** Check the connecting rod for twist.

#1 _____   #5 _____

#2 _____   #6 _____

#3 _____   #7 _____

#4 _____   #8 _____

OK _____   NOT OK _____

[Illustration labeled: SURFACE PLATE, BEND INDICATOR, CONNECTING ROD, CONTACT BARS]

_____ **2.** If not OK, were they able to be straightened? **Yes** _____   **No** _____

_____ **3.** Install the rod caps and torque to specification.

> **NOTE:** If new replacement connecting rod bolts are going to be used, press in new bolts *before* reconditioning the connecting rod.

_____ **4.** Measure the roundness of the big end of the rod: _____ (should be less than 0.001")

_____ **5.** Adjust the rod gauge to zero for the proper rod size.

_____ **6.** Remove the connecting rod caps and grind 0.001" - 0.002" from the mating surface of the caps.

_____ **7.** Reassemble the caps onto the rod and torque the fasteners to factory specification.

_____ **8.** Hone the inside diameter of the connecting rod back to its original diameter and within specification for out-of-round and taper.

> **HINT:** Place two rods together to help maintain a true inside diameter with less chance of creating a tapered hole.

_____ **9.** How close to actual specification were all connecting rods? _____

OK _____   NOT OK _____

147

Cylinder Block Specification/Measurement

Meets NATEF Task: (A1-A-3) Research applicable vehicle and service information. (P-1)

Name _____ **Date** _____ **Time on Task** _____

Make/Model/Year _____ **VIN** _____ **Evaluation: 4   3   2   1**

_____ **1.** Measure the main bearing bores (specification: _____):

#1 _____ #2 _____ #3 _____ #4 _____ #5 _____ #6 _____ #7 _____

_____ **2.** Specification for maximum out-of-round: _____

_____ **3.** Measure the cylinder bores for out-of-round:

	#1	#2	#3	#4	#5	#6	#7	#8
Out-of-round	____	____	____	____	____	____	____	____

OK___   NOT OK___

_____ **4.** Specification for maximum cylinder taper: _____

_____ **5.** Measure the cylinder bores for taper:

	#1	#2	#3	#4	#5	#6	#7	#8
Taper	__	___	___	___	___	___	___	___

OK___   NOT OK___

_____ **6.** Bore or hone cylinders as necessary - **Yes___   No___**

_____ **7.** Specification for flatness of block deck _____

_____ **8.** Measure flatness of the block deck _____

OK ___   NOT OK ___

148

Engine Block Inspection

Meets NATEF Task: (A1-C-2) Inspect engine block for visible cracks, passage condition, core and gallery plug condition, and surface warpage; determine necessary action. (P-2)

Name _____ Date _____ Time on Task _____

Make/Model/Year _____ VIN _____ Evaluation: 4   3   2   1

_____ **1.** Visually check the engine block for cracks.

  OK _____ **NOT OK** _____

  describe fault(s) _____
  _____
  _____
  _____

_____ **2.** Inspect block passages (coolant and oil) for condition.

  OK _____ **NOT OK** _____ describe fault(s) _____
  _____

_____ **3.** Inspect core and gallery plugs condition for signs of leakage.

  OK _____ **NOT OK** _____ describe fault(s) _____
  _____

_____ **4.** Check surface for warpage:

  A. Specification for maximum allowable warpage = _____

  B. Measured amount of warpage = _____

_____ **5.** What is the necessary action? _____
  _____

149

Cylinder Bore Measurement

Meets NATEF Task: (A1-C-3) Inspect and measure cylinder walls/sleeves for damage, wear, and ridges; determine necessary action. (P-2)

Name _____ Date _____ Time on Task _____

Make/Model/Year _____ VIN _____ Evaluation: 4 3 2 1

_____ **1.** Cylinder bore specifications = _____

_____ **2.** Measured cylinder bore:

Cylinder #1 _____   Cylinder #5 _____
Cylinder #2 _____   Cylinder #6 _____
Cylinder #3 _____   Cylinder #7 _____
Cylinder #4 _____   Cylinder #8 _____

OK _____   **NOT OK** _____

_____ **3.** Maximum out-of-round specification = _____

_____ **4.** Measured out-of-round:

Cylinder #1 _____   Cylinder #5 _____
Cylinder #2 _____   Cylinder #6 _____
Cylinder #3 _____   Cylinder #7 _____
Cylinder #4 _____   Cylinder #8 _____

OK _____   **NOT OK** _____

_____ **5.** Maximum taper specification = _____

_____ **6.** Measured taper:

Cylinder #1 _____   Cylinder #5 _____
Cylinder #2 _____   Cylinder #6 _____
Cylinder #3 _____   Cylinder #7 _____
Cylinder #4 _____   Cylinder #8 _____

OK _____   **NOT OK** _____

_____ **7.** What is the necessary action? _____

150

Cylinder Bore Deglazing

Meets NATEF Task: (A1-C-4) Deglaze and clean cylinder walls. (P-2)

Name _____ Date _____ Time on Task _____

Make/Model/Year _____ VIN _____ Evaluation: 4 3 2 1

A deglazing hone is designed to remove the hard surface glaze in the cylinder. A deglazing hone is flexible so that it can follow the shape of the cylinder and cannot be used to straighten the cylinder.

_____ **1.** Completely disassemble the engine block.

_____ **2.** Measure the cylinder for out-of round.

Maximum out-of-round specification = _____
Actual out-of-round:

cylinder #1 _____   cylinder #5 _____
cylinder #2 _____   cylinder #6 _____
cylinder #3 _____   cylinder #7 _____
cylinder #4 _____   cylinder #8 _____

OK _____   **NOT OK** _____

_____ **3.** Measure the cylinder for taper.

Specifications = _____
Actual cylinder taper:

cylinder #1 _____   cylinder #5 _____
cylinder #2 _____   cylinder #6 _____
cylinder #3 _____   cylinder #7 _____
cylinder #4 _____   cylinder #8 _____

OK _____   **NOT OK** _____

CROSS-HATCH PATTERN

50° ANGLE

_____ **4.** If both cylinder taper and out-of-round measurements are within factory specifications, select a deglazing hone of the proper size with a 220 or 280 grit stone.

_____ **5.** Install the hone into an electric drill motor and hone the cylinders being sure to use the proper coolant/lubricant specified by the manufacturer of the hone.

_____ **6.** After honing, be sure to wash the block with soap or detergent to thoroughly clean all of the honing grit from the block.

151

Camshaft Bearing Inspection

Meets NATEF Task: (A1-C-5) Inspect and measure camshaft bearings; determine necessary action. (P-3)

Name _____ Date _____ Time on Task _____

Make/Model/Year _____ VIN _____ Evaluation: 4 3 2 1

_____ **1.** Check service information for the exact procedures and specifications when checking camshaft bearings.

     a. Recommended procedures: _____

                               _____

     b. Specifications: _____

                               _____

_____ **2.** Based on the inspection and measurements, what is the necessary action?

            _____

            _____

            _____

            _____

            _____

            _____

152

Piston-to-Bore Clearance

Meets NATEF Task: (A1-C-11) Determine piston-to-bore clearance. (P-2)

Name _____ Date _____ Time on Task _____

Make/Model/Year _____ VIN _____ Evaluation: 4 3 2 1

_____ **1.** Check service information for the recommended procedures to follow to determine the piston-to-bore clearance. Describe the specified procedures. _____

_____

_____ **2.** What is the specified piston-to-bore clearance? _____

_____ **3.** Measure the piston-to-bore clearance on all cylinders:

Cylinder #1 _____ OK ____ NOT OK ____

Cylinder #2 _____ OK ____ NOT OK ____

Cylinder #3 _____ OK ____ NOT OK ____

Cylinder #4 _____ OK ____ NOT OK ____

Cylinder #5 _____ OK ____ NOT OK ____

Cylinder #6 _____ OK ____ NOT OK ____

Cylinder #7 _____ OK ____ NOT OK ____

Cylinder #8 _____ OK ____ NOT OK ____

153

Camshaft Bearings

Meets NATEF Task: (A1-B-13) Inspect camshaft bearing surface for wear, damage, out-of-round, and alignment; determine necessary action. (P-2)

Name _____ Date _____ Time on Task _____

Make/Model/Year _____ VIN _____ Evaluation: 4   3   2   1

_____ **1.** Check service information to determine the specified procedures and specifications for measuring camshaft bearings.

_____

_____

_____ **2.** Visually inspect the camshaft bearings for damage and excessive wear.

OK _____   NOT OK _____

Describe faults: _____

_____

_____ **3.** Measure the camshaft bearings and compare to specifications.

Front bearing	Diameter = _____	Specifications = _____
	Out of round = _____	Specifications = _____
Second bearing	Diameter = _____	Specifications = _____
	Out of round = _____	Specifications = _____
Third bearing	Diameter = _____	Specifications = _____
	Out of round = _____	Specifications = _____
Fourth bearing	Diameter = _____	Specifications = _____
	Out of round = _____	Specifications = _____
Fifth bearing	Diameter = _____	Specifications = _____
	Out of round = _____	Specifications = _____

_____ **4.** Based on the inspection and measurements of the camshaft bearings, what is the necessary action?

_____

_____

154

Crankshaft Specification and Measurement

Meets NATEF Task: (A1-C-6) Inspect crankshaft for straightness, journal damage, keyway damage; determine necessary action (P-1)

Name _____ Date _____ Time on Task _____

Make/Model/Year _____ VIN _____ Evaluation: 4 3 2 1

Engine _____ VIN _____

Check service information to obtain the specifications.

_____ 1. Forged _____ Cast _____ Unknown _____

_____ 2. Number of main bearings: _____

_____ 3. Thrust taken by which bearing? _____

_____ 4. Main bearing journal diameter specification: _____

_____ 5. Maximum main bearing journal out-of-round or taper: _____

_____ 6. Connecting rod bearing journal diameter specification: _____

           Actual measured connecting rod bearing journal diameter: _____

_____ 7. Maximum specified rod bearing journal out-of-round or taper: _____

           Actual measured rod-bearing journal out-of-round: _____

_____ 8. Connecting rod side clearance specification: _____

           Actual measured connection rod side clearance: _____

_____ 9. Crankshaft endplay specification: _____

           Actual measured crankshaft endplay: _____

_____ 10. What is the necessary action? _____

_____

155

Crankshaft Inspection

Meets NATEF Task: (A1-C-6) Inspect crankshaft for straightness, journal damage, keyway damage; determine necessary action (P-1)

Name _____ Date _____ Time on Task _____

Make/Model/Year _____ VIN _____ Evaluation: 4 3 2 1

_____ **1.** Check service information for the crankshaft specifications and inspection procedure.

_____

_____ **2.** Inspect crankshaft for straightness. **OK** ____ **NOT OK** ____

_____ **3.** Check crankshaft journals for damage. **OK** ____ **NOT OK** ____

_____ **4.** Check the crankshaft keyway for damage. **OK** ____ **NOT OK** ____

_____ **5.** Check the crankshaft thrust flange and sealing surfaces condition.

OK ____   **NOT OK** ____

_____ **6.** Visually check the crankshaft for cracks. **OK** ____ **NOT OK** ____

_____ **7.** Measure crankshaft journals and determine if worn.

Main bearing journals: ____ ____ ____ ____ ____ ____

Rod bearing journals: ____ ____ ____ ____ ____

_____ **8.** Based on the results of the inspection and measurement of the crankshaft, what is the necessary action?

_____

_____

156

Main and Rod Bearings

Meets NATEF Task: (A1-C-7) Inspect main and connecting rod bearings for damage and wear; determine necessary action. (P2)

Name _____ Date _____ Time on Task _____

Make/Model/Year _____ VIN _____ Evaluation: 4 3 2 1

_____ 1. Check service information to determine the specified procedures and specifications for main and connecting rod bearings.

_____

_____ 2. Visually check the main and connecting rod bearings for damage or excessive wear.

OK _____ NOT OK _____ Describe faults: _____

_____ 3. Measure the main bearings and compare to factory specifications.

Front main bearing = _____ Specifications = _____
Second main bearing = _____ Specifications = _____
Third main bearing = _____ Specifications = _____
Fourth main bearing = _____ Specifications = _____
Fifth main bearing = _____ Specifications = _____
Sixth main bearing = _____ Specifications = _____
Seventh main bearing = _____ Specifications = _____
Eighth main bearing = _____ Specifications = _____

_____ 4. Record connecting rod bearing measurements and compare to factory specifications.

Front connecting rod bearing = _____ Specifications = _____
Second connecting rod bearing = _____ Specifications = _____
Third connecting rod bearing = _____ Specifications = _____
Fourth connecting rod bearing = _____ Specifications = _____
Fifth connecting rod bearing = _____ Specifications = _____
Sixth connecting rod bearing = _____ Specifications = _____
Seventh connecting rod bearing = _____ Specifications = _____
Eighth connecting rod bearing = _____ Specifications = _____

_____ 5. Check the main bearing end play and compare to factory specifications.

End play = _____ Specifications = _____

_____ 6. Based on the inspection and measurements of the main and connecting rod bearings, what is the necessary action (include the proper selection of bearings)?

_____

157

Piston and Bearing Wear Patterns

Meets NATEF Task: (A1-C-8) Identify piston and bearing wear patterns that indicate connecting rod alignment and main bearing bore problems; determine necessary action. (P-3)

Name _____ Date _____ Time on Task _____

Make/Model/Year _____ VIN _____ Evaluation: 4 3 2 1

_____ 1. Check service information to determine procedures and specifications for connecting rod and main bearing bore alignment.

_____

_____

_____ 2. Visually inspect the piston skirts for *diagonal wear*, which could indicate a bent connecting rod.

OK _____ **NOT OK** _____

_____ 3. Visually inspect the connecting rod bearings for abnormal wear patterns.

OK _____ **NOT OK** _____ Describe faults: _____

_____

_____ 4. Visually inspect the main bearings for abnormal wear patterns.

OK _____ **NOT OK** _____ Describe faults: _____

_____

_____ 5. Using the specified procedure and equipment, check the connecting rods for proper alignment.

OK _____ **NOT OK** _____ Describe faults: _____

_____

_____ 6. Using the specified procedure and equipment, check the main bearing bore for proper alignment.

OK _____ **NOT OK** _____ Describe faults: _____

_____

158

Crankshaft Vibration Damper

Meets NATEF Task: (A1-C-14) Remove, inspect or replace crankshaft vibration damper (harmonic balancer). (P-2)

Name _____ Date _____ Time on Task _____

Make/Model/Year _____ VIN _____ Evaluation: 4 3 2 1

_____ **1.** Check service information for the specified inspection and installation procedure.

_____

_____

_____

_____

_____ **2.** Visually check the condition of the crankshaft vibration damper (harmonic balancer) including:

    a. Rubber connection between the inner and outer rings

    b. Nose area for wear from the front seal

    OK _____ **NOT OK** _____ Describe faults: _____

_____

_____ **3.** Check service information for the specified torque specifications for the crankshaft vibration damper retaining bolt.   Torque specification = _____

_____ **4.** Install the crankshaft vibration damper and tighten the retaining bolt to factory specifications.

159

Auxiliary and Balance Shafts

Meets NATEF Task: (A1-C-13) Inspect auxiliary (balance, intermediate, idler, counter balance or silencer) shaft(s); inspect; determine necessary action. (P2)

Name _____ Date _____ Time on Task _____

Make/Model/Year _____ VIN _____ Evaluation: 4 3 2 1

_____ **1.** Check service information to determine the specified checking procedure and specifications for auxiliary shafts and bearings.

_____

_____

_____

_____ **2.** Visually check the auxiliary shaft(s) and bearings for damage and excessive wear.

OK _____ **NOT OK** _____ Describe faults: _____

_____

_____ **3.** Based on visual inspection and specified checking procedures, what is the necessary action?

_____

_____

_____

_____

_____ **4.** Check service information for the correct timing during the installation of counter balance or silencer shafts. Show instructor the correctly installed shaft.

Instructor's OK _____

CAMSHAFT SPROCKET

TIMING CHAIN

BALANCE SHAFT

BALANCE SHAFT

BALANCE SHAFT CHAIN

BALANCE SHAFT SPROCKET

CRANKSHAFT SPROCKET

160

Gaskets and Sealants

Meets NATEF Task: (A1-A-13) Install engine covers using gaskets, seals, and sealers as required. (P-1)

Name _____ **Date** _____ **Time on Task** _____

Make/Model/Year _____ **VIN** _____ **Evaluation:** 4 3 2 1

Proper engine assembly requires the use of gaskets and sealants. Consult the gasket packaging or service manual information and answer the following:

_____ 1. What types of head gaskets are being used?

       _____ embossed steel shim
       _____ perforated steel core
       _____ multilayered steel
       _____ other or unknown (describe) _____

_____ 2. Is sealant such as RTV silicone required during the assembly of the engine and if so, where? (Check all that apply.)

       _____ at the ends of the intake manifold
       _____ at the corners of the intake manifold
       _____ oil pan
       _____ timing chain cover
       _____ other (describe) _____

_____ 3. What type of gasket is used for the oil pan gasket?

       _____ RTV
       _____ cork
       _____ cork/rubber
       _____ synthetic rubber
       _____ other (describe) _____

_____ 4. What type of gasket is used for the valve (cylinder head) cover?

       _____ RTV
       _____ cork
       _____ cork/rubber
       _____ synthetic rubber
       _____ other (describe) _____
       _____

161

Pistons and Rods Balancing

Meets NATEF Task: (Not specified by NATEF)

Name _____ Date _____ Time on Task _____

Make/Model/Year _____ VIN _____ Evaluation: 4 3 2 1

_____ **1.** Recondition all connection rods.

> **NOTE:** Balancing should only be attempted after the rods have been reconditioned.

_____ **2.** Weigh all of the pistons.

1. _____   5. _____
2. _____   6. _____
3. _____   7. _____
4. _____   8. _____

_____ **3.** Which is the lightest? _____

_____ **4.** Balance the piston weight by grinding material from the piston balance pads or pin boss pads to match the lightest piston.

All pistons are now within _____ grams   **OK** _____   **NOT OK** _____

_____ **5.** Weigh all the rods. (small end/big end)

1. _____/_____   5. _____/_____
2. _____/_____   6. _____/_____
3. _____/_____   7. _____/_____
4. _____/_____   8. _____/_____

_____ **6.** Grind material from the balancing pad(s) to match the weight of all the connecting rods to match the lightest. All rods are within _____ grams.

OK _____   **NOT OK** _____

162

Crankshaft Balancing

Meets NATEF Task: (Not specified by NATEF)

Name _____ **Date** _____ **Time on Task** _____

Make/Model/Year _____ **VIN** _____ **Evaluation:** 4 3 2 1

_____ 1. To determine the amount of bob weight (if needed), measure the weight of the following:

piston with pin:	_____	grams
locks:	_____	grams
rings:	_____	grams
bearings:	_____	grams
rod big end:	_____	grams
small end:	_____	grams
oil weight:	_____	grams (usually 3 to 6 grams)

NOTE: Even though the balance machine will often calculate the bob weight, the following formula is used:

Piston weight
Pin weight
Locks weight
Rings weight
Small end of rod weight
    TOTAL = _____ X 2 (if a V-8) = reciprocating weight

Reciprocating weight X 50% (balance factor) = calculated reciprocating weight.

Rotating wt. = calculated reciprocating wt. + insert weight + rod big end weight X 2.

Bob weight = calculated reciprocating weight + rotating weight.

_____ 2. Install the harmonic balancer and flywheel (flexplate) if externally balanced.

_____ 3. Amount of weight needed to be added or removed to balance = _____

_____ 4. Balance (should be within 3 grams).   **OK** _____   **NOT OK** _____

163

Combustion Chamber Volume Test

Meets NATEF Task: Not specified by NATEF

Name _____ **Date** _____ **Time on Task** _____

Make/Model/Year _____ **VIN** _____ **Evaluation: 4   3   2   1**

This procedure should be performed before machining the cylinder head(s) to check compression ratio.

_____ **1.** Install the specified spark plug in the plug hole.

_____ **2.** Install the valves.

_____ **3.** Apply a thin layer of grease to the edge around the combustion chamber to create a seal between the plastic plate and the head.

_____ **4.** Place the plastic plate over the combustion chamber and place the hole in the plate near the edge.

_____ **5.** Fill the burette with mineral spirits.

> **HINT:** Automotive transmission fluid (ATF) could also be used.

_____ **6.** Adjust the fluid level to zero (use the lower portion or meniscus of the fluid as the measuring point).

_____ **7.** Place the burette over the hole and slowly add liquid until all the air has escaped and the combustion chamber is filled with fluid. Read the volumes of each cylinder and record.

Cylinder #1 _____   Cylinder #5 _____

Cylinder #2 _____   Cylinder #6 _____

Cylinder #3 _____   Cylinder #7 _____

Cylinder #4 _____   Cylinder #8 _____

_____ **8.** Remove material around the spark plug to achieve equal volume.

164

We Support
NATEF

Torque Specification

Meets NATEF Task: (A1-A-3) Research applicable vehicle and service information. (P-1)

Name _____ **Date** _____ **Time on Task** _____

Make/Model/Year _____ **VIN** _____ **Evaluation:** 4   3   2   1

Engine _____ **VIN** _____

Determine the tightening torque specifications for the following.

_____ **1.** Main Bearing caps: _____

_____ **2.** Connecting rod bearing caps: _____

_____ **3.** Oil pump: _____

_____ **4.** Cylinder head(s): _____

_____ **5.** Flywheel/flexplate: _____

_____ **6.** Camshaft sprocket: _____

_____ **7.** Oil pan: _____

_____ **8.** Exhaust manifold: _____

_____ **9.** Intake manifold: _____

_____ **10.** Cylinder head covers (valve covers): _____

_____ **11.** Water pump: _____

_____ **12.** Spark Plugs: _____

165

Cylinder Head Replacement

Meets NATEF Task: (A1-B-1) Remove cylinder head; inspect gasket condition; install cylinder head and gasket; tighten according to manufacturer's specifications. (P-1)

Name _____ Date _____ Time on Task _____

Make/Model/Year _____ VIN _____ Evaluation: 4 3 2 1

The cylinder head gasket will have to be replaced if there is one or more of the following problems:

- An internal coolant leak into the combustion chamber
- An external oil or coolant leak at the head gasket

_____ 1. Allow the engine to cool and drain the coolant into a suitable container to be disposed of properly or recycled.

_____ 2. Remove the air cleaner assembly and other components as necessary to gain access to the cylinder head and retaining bolts. Items that required removal:

_____ _____ _____
_____ _____ _____

_____ 3. Remove the intake manifold and cylinder head(s) following the tightening torque sequence in reverse.

_____ 4. Clean all gasket surfaces.

> **CAUTION:** Do not use fiber abrasive pads to clean the gasket surfaces. Particles of the fiber disc can get into the engine and cause serious engine wear and damage. Do not use steel tools to scrape gaskets from an aluminum surface.

_____ 5. Install the replacement cylinder head and intake manifold gaskets following the vehicle manufacturer's recommended procedure.

_____ 6. Torque the retaining bolts to factory specifications. _____

Intake manifold bolt torque specification = _____
Cylinder head bolt torque specification = _____

_____ 7. Reassemble the top of the engine.

_____ 8. Refill the cooling system with new coolant and check for leaks and proper engine operation.

> **CAUTION:** Be sure to open cooling system bleeder valves(s), if equipped, to avoid trapping air.

166

Timing Gears/Chain/Belt Installation

Meets NATEF Task: (A1-B-11) Inspect and replace camshaft and drive belt/chain (includes checking drive gear wear and backlash, end play, sprocket and chain wear. (P-1)

Name _____ Date _____ Time on Task _____

Make/Model/Year _____ VIN _____ Evaluation: 4 3 2 1

The valve opening and closing has to be in the correct relationship to the crankshaft position to ensure proper engine operation.

_____ 1. What is the type of valve train?

        _____ timing gears
        _____ single chain
        _____ primary and secondary chain
        _____ chain and belt
        _____ belt
        _____ other (describe) _____

_____ 2. Describe the factory recommended timing gear/chain/belt installation instructions:

        _____
        _____
        _____
        _____

_____ 3. Is the engine timed with #1 cylinder at TDC compression stroke?

        _____ **Yes**
        _____ **No** (describe) _____
                   _____

_____ 4. Describe the timing marks.

        _____ dots
        _____ arrows
        _____ dark or light chain links
        _____ other (describe) _____
                  _____

167

Main Bearing Installation

Meets NATEF Task: (A1-C-7) Inspect main and connecting rod bearings for damage and wear; determine necessary action. (P-2)

Name _____ Date _____ Time on Task _____

Make/Model/Year _____ VIN _____ Evaluation: 4 3 2 1

_____ **1.** Check service information for the recommended procedure to follow for inspecting main and rod bearings (describe). _____

_____

_____

_____ **2.** Remove each bearing cap and compare the width of the plastic gauging material to the paper scale printed on the gauge package (should be within 0.001-0.003 in. for most engines):

Rod Bearing Clearance

Front bearing clearance _____   #1 rod _____

#2   bearing clearance _____   #2 rod _____

#3   bearing clearance _____   #3 rod _____

#4   bearing clearance _____   #4 rod _____

#5   bearing clearance _____   #5 rod _____

#6   bearing clearance _____   #6 rod _____

#7   bearing clearance _____   #7 rod _____

Specification range: _____ to _____   #8 rod _____

_____ **3.** Based on the inspection and measurements, what is the necessary action? _____

_____

_____

_____

168

Piston Fitting

Meets NATEF Task: (A1-C-11) Determine piston-to-bore clearance.
(P-2)

Name _____ Date _____ Time on Task _____

Make/Model/Year _____ VIN _____ Evaluation: 4 3 2 1

_____ **1.** Check service information for the specified piston-to-cylinder wall clearance.

_____

_____ **2.** With a micrometer, measure the piston skirt diameter.

Specification = _____

Actual = Piston #1 _____   Piston #5 _____

Piston #2 _____   Piston #6 _____

Piston #3 _____   Piston #7 _____

Piston #4 _____   Piston #8 _____

(Hint: Label the size on the pistons using a marker for identification.)

_____ **3.** With a telescoping gauge and micrometer measure the smallest diameter of the cylinder.

Cylinder #1 _____   Cylinder #5 _____

Cylinder #2 _____   Cylinder #6 _____

Cylinder #3 _____   Cylinder #7 _____

Cylinder #4 _____   Cylinder #8 _____

_____ **4.** Select the largest diameter piston and, using a thickness gauge, fit the piston to the largest diameter cylinder. Continue selecting pistons and fit each to the cylinder that results in the best fit with the correct clearance (usually between 0.001 and 0.003 in).

_____ **5.** Match the cylinder number on the top of the selected piston for each cylinder.

Cylinder #1 uses piston # _____   Cylinder #5 uses piston # _____

Cylinder #2 uses piston # _____   Cylinder #6 uses piston # _____

Cylinder #3 uses piston # _____   Cylinder #7 uses piston # _____

Cylinder #4 uses piston # _____   Cylinder #8 uses piston # _____

169

Cylinder Head Replacement

Meets NATEF Task: (A1-B-2) Install cylinder heads and gaskets; tighten according to the manufacturer's specifications and procedures. (P-1)

Name _____ **Date** _____ **Time on Task** _____

Make/Model/Year _____ **VIN** _____ **Evaluation:** 4 3 2 1

The cylinder head gasket will have to be replaced if there is one or more of the following problems:

- An internal coolant leak into the combustion chamber
- An external oil or coolant leak at the head gasket

_____ **1.** Allow the engine to cool, and drain the coolant into a suitable container to be disposed of properly or recycled.

_____ **2.** Remove the air cleaner assembly and other components as necessary to gain access to the cylinder head and retaining bolts. Items that required removal:

_____ _____ _____
_____ _____ _____

_____ **3.** Remove the intake manifold and cylinder head(s) following the tightening torque sequence in reverse.

_____ **4.** Clean all gasket surfaces.

> **CAUTION:** Do not use fiber abrasive pads to clean the gasket surfaces. Particles of the fiber disc can get into the engine and cause serious engine wear and damage. Do not use steel tools to scrape gaskets from an aluminum surface.

_____ **5.** Install the replacement cylinder head and intake manifold gaskets following the vehicle manufacturer's recommended procedure.

_____ **6.** Torque the retaining bolts to factory specifications. _____

Intake manifold bolt torque specification = _____
Cylinder head bolt torque specification = _____

_____ **7.** Reassemble the top of the engine.

_____ **8.** Refill the cooling system with new coolant and check for leaks and proper engine operation.

> **CAUTION:** Be sure to open cooling system bleeder valves(s), if equipped, to avoid trapping air.

170

Camshaft Bearings Installation

Meets NATEF Task: (Not specified by NATEF)

Name _____   Date _____   Time on Task _____

Make/Model/Year _____   VIN _____   Evaluation: 4 3 2 1

_____ 1. Be sure the engine block is thoroughly cleaned and place the block upside down for best visibility of the camshaft bearing installation.

_____ 2. Read, understand, and follow the instructions that come in the box with the cam bearings. Be sure to mark the location of each bearing with a felt marker, if necessary, starting with the rear bearing.

_____ 3. Orient the cam bearing so the oil feed hole aligns with the oil hole in the block (cam bearing bore).

_____ 4. Use a cam bearing installation tool and select the proper size bearing driver. Starting at the rear, position the bearing in the bore and gently tap the bearing into the bore. Check for proper alignment of the oil feed hole.

_____ 5. After confirming that the oil feed holes line up, continue to drive the bearing shell into the cam bearing bore.

_____ 6. Repeat the procedure for the rest of the cam bearing and end with the bearing closest to the front of the engine.

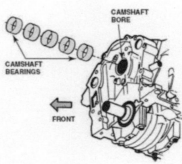

171

Crankshaft Inspection

Meets NATEF Task: (A1-C-7) Inspect crankshaft; determine necessary action. (P-2)

___

Name _____ Date _____ Time on Task _____

Make/Model/Year _____ VIN _____ Evaluation: 4   3   2   1

_____ **1.** Check service information and determine the specified methods to use to check the
condition of the crankshaft (describe procedure). _____

_____

_____

_____

_____ **2.** Check all that apply:

_____ Straightness   **OK** _____ **NOT OK**_____

(describe) _____

_____ Keyway condition   **OK** _____ **NOT OK**_____

(describe) _____

_____ Journal wear condition   **OK** _____ **NOT OK**_____

(describe) _____

_____ Cracks and damage   **OK** _____ **NOT OK**_____

(describe) _____

_____ **3.** Based on the inspection, what is the necessary action? _____

_____

172

Main Bearing Installation

Meets NATEF Task: (A1-C-8) Inspect main and road bearings; determine necessary action.
(P-2)

Name _____ Date _____ Time on Task _____

Make/Model/Year _____ VIN _____ Evaluation: 4 3 2 1

_____ 1. Check service information for the recommended procedure to follow for inspecting main and rod bearings (describe). _____

_____

_____

_____ 2. Remove each bearing cap and compare the width of the plastic gauging material to the paper scale printed on the gauge package (should be within 0.001-0.003 in. for most engines):

		Rod Bearing Clearance
Front bearing clearance _____		#1 rod _____
#2 bearing clearance _____		#2 rod _____
#3 bearing clearance _____		#3 rod _____
#4 bearing clearance _____		#4 rod _____
#5 bearing clearance _____		#5 rod _____
#6 bearing clearance _____		#6 rod _____
#7 bearing clearance _____		#7 rod _____
Specification range: _____ to _____		#8 rod _____

_____ 3. Based on the inspection and measurements, what is the necessary action? _____

_____

_____

_____

173

Auxiliary Shaft Inspection

Meets NATEF Task: (A1-C-13) Inspect auxiliary shaft; determine necessary action. (P-2)

Name _____ Date _____ Time on Task _____

Make/Model/Year _____ VIN _____ Evaluation: 4 3 2 1

_____ 1. Check service information for the specified methods and procedures to follow when inspecting auxiliary shafts, such as balance shafts and bearings (describe procedure).

_____

_____

_____

_____ 2. What type of auxiliary (balance) shaft is used? _____

_____

_____ 3. What type of bearing is used to support the shaft(s)? _____

_____

_____ 4. Based on the inspection, what is the necessary action? _____

_____

_____

174

Inspect Crankshaft Vibration Damper

Meets NATEF Task: (A1-C-14) Remove, inspect or replace crankshaft vibration damper (harmonic balancer). (P-2)

Name _____ Date _____ Time on Task _____

Make/Model/Year _____ VIN _____ Evaluation: 4 3 2 1

_____ **1.** Check service information for the exact procedure and tools needed to remove and install the crankshaft vibration damper. Describe the procedures and list the tools needed.

_____

_____

Tools needed: _____

_____

_____ **2.** Check service information and determine what to look for during the inspection of the crankshaft vibration damper (describe procedures). _____

_____

_____

_____

175

Assemble Engine Block

Meets NATEF Task: (A1-C-15) Assemble engine block. (P-1)

Name _____ Date _____ Time on Task _____

Make/Model/Year _____ VIN _____ Evaluation: 4 3 2 1

_____ **1.** Check service information for the specified procedures to follow when assembling the engine block. Describe specified procedures. _____

_____

_____

_____ **2.** List the tools specified to be needed to assemble the engine block.

_____

_____

_____

_____

176

We Support
NATEF

Oil Pump Inspection

Meets NATEF Task: (A1-D-2) Inspect oil pump; perform necessary action. (P-2)

Name _____ **Date** _____ **Time on Task** _____

Make/Model/Year _____ **VIN** _____ **Evaluation:** 4 3 2 1

_____ **1.** Check service information for the specified methods and measurements required to be made to determine the condition of the oil pump. _____

_____

_____

_____

_____

_____ **2.** Based on the inspection, what is the necessary action? _____

_____

_____

_____

177

We Support
ASE NATEF

Inspect and Replace Engine Cooling Hoses

Meets NATEF Task: (A1-D-5) Inspect and replace engine cooling and heater hoses. (P-1)

Name _____ **Date** _____ **Time on Task** _____

Make/Model/Year _____ **VIN** _____ **Evaluation:** 4 3 2 1

_____ **1.** Check service information and determine the exact procedures to follow when replacing engine cooling and heater hoses (describe procedure). _____

_____

_____

_____

_____ **2.** What is the specified procedure to follow to burp trapped air out of the cooling system?

_____

_____

_____

178

Replace Thermostat

Meets NATEF Task: (A1-D-6) Inspect, test, and replace thermostat. (P-1)

Name _____ Date _____ Time on Task _____

Make/Model/Year _____ VIN _____ Evaluation: 4 3 2 1

_____ **1.** Check service information and determine the recommended thermostat testing and replacement procedures.

_____

_____

> **CAUTION:** Do not remove the pressure cap until the engine has cooled. The sudden drop in pressure that occurs when the cap is removed can cause the coolant to boil and cause serious burns from the escaping hot coolant.

_____ **2.** Drain the cooling system into a suitable container, down to below the level of the thermostat.

_____ **3.** Remove the thermostat housing bolts and housing.

_____ **4.** What other components had to be removed to gain access to the thermostat housing?

_____

_____

_____

_____ **5.** Remove the thermostat and discard the gasket. Clean both gasket-sealing surfaces.

Instructor's OK _____

_____ **6.** Install the replacement thermostat into the recesses in the housing bore.

_____ **7.** Install a new gasket and reinstall the thermostat housing and retaining bolts.

_____ **8.** Torque the thermostat housing to factory specification.

Thermostat housing bolt torque specification = _____

_____ **9.** Refill the cooling system with new coolant.
> **CAUTION:** Be sure to open the cooling system bleeder valves(s), if equipped, to avoid trapping air.

_____ **10.** Install the radiator pressure cap and start the engine. Check for leaks and proper cooling system operation.

179

Replace Water Pump

Meets NATEF Task: (A1-D-8) Inspect and replace water pump. (P-2)

Name _____ Date _____ Time on Task _____

Make/Model/Year _____ VIN _____ Evaluation: 4 3 2 1

_____ **1.** Check service information for the recommended procedures to inspect and replace the water pump (describe recommended procedures). _____

_____

_____

_____

_____ **2.** What are the torque specifications for the water pump fasteners? _____

_____

180

Remove and Replace Radiator

Meets NATEF Task: (A1-D-9) Remove and replace radiator. (P-2)

Name _____ **Date** _____ **Time on Task** _____

Make/Model/Year _____ **VIN** _____ **Evaluation: 4   3   2   1**

_____ **1.** Check service information for the recommended procedures for replacing the radiator
(describe recommended procedures). _____

_____

_____

_____

_____ **2.** What is the specified torque specification for the radiator attaching fasteners? _____

_____

181

Inspect Cooling Fan

Meets NATEF Task: (A1-D-10) Inspect and test fan(s) (electrical or mechanical), fan clutch, fan shroud, and air dams.. (P-1)

Name _____ Date _____ Time on Task _____

Make/Model/Year _____ VIN _____ Evaluation: 4 3 2 1

_____ **1.** Check service information for the specified procedures to follow to diagnose engine cooling fan(s) (describe the specified procedures). _____

_____

_____

_____

_____ **2.** What is the type of cooling fan? _____

_____ **3.** Check related components such as the fan shroud and air dam.

   OK ____ **NOT OK** ____ Describe the fault: _____

_____

Remove and Install Engine

Meets NATEF Task: (A1-A-12) Remove and install engine.
(P-2)

Name _____ **Date** _____ **Time on Task** _____

Make/Model/Year _____ **VIN** _____ **Evaluation:** 4 3 2 1

_____ **1.** Check service information for the recommended steps to follow when removing and

installing an engine. List the steps. _____

_____

_____

_____

183

Valve Cover Gasket Replacement

Meets NATEF Task: (A1-A-13) Install engine covers, using gaskets and seals as required.
(P-1)

Name _____ Date _____ Time on Task _____

Make/Model/Year _____ VIN _____ Evaluation: 4 3 2 1

_____ 1. Remove the air cleaner assembly and other brackets, wiring, hoses, or components to allow access to the valve cover(s). Be sure to mark the location of all wiring and hoses so they can be correctly replaced.

_____ 2. List the parts and components that have to be removed to gain access to the valve covers.

_____ _____ _____ _____

_____ _____ _____ _____

_____ 3. Remove the valve (rocker arm or cylinder head) cover retaining bolts and remove the cover.

_____ 4. Type of gasket used?

_____ RTV _____ cork _____ cork/rubber _____ rubber
_____ other (specify) _____

_____ 5. Clean both gasket surfaces thoroughly.

_____ 6. Install a new gasket. What type of replacement gasket is being used?

_____ RTV _____ cork _____ cork/rubber _____ rubber
_____ other (specify) _____

_____ 7. Torque the valve cover retaining bolts to factory specifications.

Valve cover bolt tightening torque specification = _____

_____ 8. Complete the repair by reassembling the components previously removed.

_____ 9. Start the engine and check for proper engine operation and look for oil leaks from the valve cover.

OK _____ NOT OK _____ Describe the problem: _____

184

We Support
NATEF

Timing Belt Replacement

Meets NATEF Task: (A1-B-13) Inspect and replace timing belts; adjust as necessary. (P-1)

Name _____ Date _____ Time on Task _____

Make/Model/Year _____ VIN _____ Evaluation: 4 3 2 1

_____ 1. Allow the engine to cool, and then remove the radiator pressure cap.

> **CAUTION:** Do not remove the pressure cap until the engine has cooled. The sudden drop in pressure that occurs when the cap is removed can cause the coolant to boil and cause serious burns from the escaping hot coolant.

_____ 2. Drain the cooling system coolant into a suitable container and dispose it properly or recycle it. Remove the accessory drive belt(s). Remove other components and brackets necessary to remove the water pump from the engine. The parts that needed to be removed included:

   _____   _____
   _____   _____

_____ 3. Remove the timing belt covers.

_____ 4. Loosen or remove the timing belt tensioner(s).

_____ 5. Many experts recommend that the following items be replaced whenever replacing a timing belt to prevent premature failure due to contamination with oil or coolant.

   water pump, camshaft seals (if equipped), crankshaft front seal, tensioner(s)

_____ 6. What parts were replaced? _____ _____

   _____   _____

_____ 7. Install a new timing belt and double check that the valve timing is correct.

_____ 8. Reassemble the front of the engine.

_____ 9. Refill the cooling system with new coolant.

> **CAUTION:** Be sure to open the cooling system bleeder valves(s), if equipped, to avoid trapping air.

_____ 10. Install the radiator pressure cap and start the engine. Check for leaks and proper cooling system operation.

We Support
NATEF

Timing Chain Replacement

Meets NATEF Task: (A1-B-13) Inspect and replace timing belts; adjust as necessary. (P-1)

Name _____ Date _____ Time on Task _____

Make/Model/Year _____ VIN _____ Evaluation: 4 3 2 1

The timing chain used in many overhead valve (OHV) engines should be replaced whenever there is excessive slack (over 8° as measured at the crankshaft) or noise caused by the loose chain hitting the timing chain cover.

_____ 1. Drain the cooling system coolant into a suitable container and dispose of it properly or recycle it.

_____ 2. Remove the accessory drive belt and pulley from the harmonic balancer (vibration damper).

> **NOTE:** On many vehicles it is often necessary to remove the radiator to provide the room necessary to replace the timing chain.

_____ 3. Remove the harmonic balancer retaining bolt and use a puller (if needed) to remove the harmonic balancer and the timing chain cover.

> **NOTE:** On many engines such as the small block Chevrolet V-8, the front of the oil pan must be loosened to be able to remove the timing chain cover.

_____ 4. Remove the timing chain and both the crankshaft and camshaft sprockets.

Type of chain used originally = _____
Type of replacement chain = _____

_____ 5. Install the replacement timing chain and sprockets. Check that the timing marks align.

_____ 6. Reassemble the front of the engine and torque all fasteners to factory specifications.

Timing chain cover bolt torque specification = _____
Harmonic balancer retaining bolt torque specification = _____
Water pump bolt torque specification = _____

_____ 7. Refill the cooling system with new coolant and check for leaks.

> **CAUTION:** Be sure to open the cooling system bleeder valves(s), if equipped, to avoid trapping air.

Engine Oil Change

Meets NATEF Task: (A1-D-13) Perform oil and filter change. (P-1)

Name _____ Date _____ Time on Task _____

Make/Model/Year _____ VIN _____ Evaluation: 4   3   2   1

_____ **1.** Check the owner's manual, service manual, or technical literature to determine the correct viscosity rating and quantity of oil needed.
      a.   recommended viscosity: SAE _____ or SAE _____
      b.   Number of quarts (liters): with the filter _____ without the filter _____
      c.   American Petroleum Institute rating (if specified) _____

_____ **2.** Filter brand and number: Brand _____ Number _____

_____ **3.** Hoist the vehicle safely. Position the oil drain unit under the drain plug and raise to a height about 1 foot under the drain plug.

_____ **4.** Select the proper size wrench and remove the drain plug and allow the oil to drain into the drain pan.
        HINT: Apply a light force against the drain plug as you rotate it out of the oil pan. Then pull the drain plug away after unthreading the plug all the way. This helps prevent getting oil all over you and the floor!

_____ **5.** After all the oil has been drained, install a new sealing washer (if needed) and install the drain plug.

_____ **6.** Move the oil drain unit under the filter and remove the old oil filter.

_____ **7.** Use a shop cloth and clean the oil filter gasket contact area on the engine block.

_____ **8.** Apply a thin coating of engine oil to the rubber gasket on the new oil filter.

_____ **9.** Install the new oil filter and hand tighten about 3/4 turn after the gasket contacts the engine block.

_____ **10.** Lower the vehicle. Install the recommended quantity of engine oil using a funnel to prevent spilling oil. Replace the oil filler cap.

_____ **11.** Start the engine and allow it to idle. The "oil" light should go out within 15 seconds.

_____ **12.** Look under the vehicle and check for leaks at the drain plug and the oil filter.

_____ **13.** Check the level of the oil again and add as necessary. **Caution:** Do not overfill!

APPENDIX

2013 NATEF Correlation Chart

MLR–Maintenance & Light Repair
AST–Auto Service Technology (Includes MLR)
MAST–Master Auto Service Technology (Includes MLR and AST)

ENGINE REPAIR (A1)							
Task	Priority	MLR	AST	MAST	Text Page #	Task Page #	
A. General: Engine Diagnosis; Removal and Reinstallation (R & R)							
1. Complete work order to include customer information, vehicle identifying information, customer concern, related service history, cause, and correction.	P-1		✓	✓	78; 85–89	15	
2. Research applicable vehicle and service information, vehicle service history, service precautions, and technical service bulletins.	P-1	✓	✓	✓	85–89	17, 19, 20, 24, 25, 31, 42, 85, 86, 114, 124, 125, 132, 142, 149, 169	
3. Verify operation of the instrument panel engine warning indicators.	P-1	✓	✓	✓	193; 305–306	45, 103	
4. Inspect engine assembly for fuel, oil, coolant, and other leaks; determine necessary action.	P-1	✓	✓	✓	302–303	90, 91, 92, 93	
5. Install engine covers using gaskets, seals, and sealers as required.	P-1	✓	✓	✓	476–480	170, 206	
6. Remove and replace timing belt; verify correct camshaft timing.	P-1	✓	✓	✓	396–398; 411–417; 512–513	137, 172, 207, 208	
7. Perform common fastener and thread repair, to include: remove broken bolt, restore internal and external threads, and repair internal threads with thread insert.	P-1	✓	✓	✓	27–30	4	
8. Inspect, remove and replace engine mounts.	P-2		✓	✓	331	106	
9. Identify hybrid vehicle internal combustion engine service precautions.	P-3	✓	✓	✓	179; 322–323	NA	
10. Remove and reinstall engine in an OBDII or newer vehicle; reconnect all attaching components and restore the vehicle to running condition.	P-3		✓	✓	330–332; 525–529	104, 105, 205	

Task	Priority	MLR	AST	MAST	Text Page #	Task Page #
B. Cylinder Head and Valve Train Diagnosis and Repair						
1. Remove cylinder head; inspect gasket condition; install cylinder head and gasket; tighten according to manufacturer's specifications and procedures.	P-1		✓	✓	332–334; 497; 508–512	115, 171
2. Clean and visually inspect a cylinder head for cracks; check gasket surface areas for warpage and surface finish; check passage condition.	P-1		✓	✓	358–362	116, 123, 182
3. Inspect pushrods, rocker arms, rocker arm pivots and shafts for wear, bending, cracks, looseness, and blocked oil passages (orifices); determine necessary action.	P-2		✓	✓	399–403	133, 134
4. Adjust valves (mechanical or hydraulic lifters).	P-1	✓	✓	✓	508–509; 514–515	136
5. Inspect and replace camshaft and drive belt/chain; includes checking drive gear wear and backlash, end play, sprocket and chain wear, overhead cam drive sprocket(s), drive belt(s), belt tension, tensioners, camshaft reluctor ring/tone-wheel, and valve timing components; verify correct camshaft timing.	P-1		✓	✓	396–398; 411–417; 512–513	137, 172, 207, 208
6. Establish camshaft position sensor indexing.	P-1		✓	✓	413	141
7. Inspect valve springs for squareness and free height comparison; determine necessary action.	P-3			✓	384	129
8. Replace valve stem seals on an assembled engine; inspect valve spring retainers, locks/keepers, and valve lock/keeper grooves; determine necessary action.	P-3			✓	384–388	126
9. Inspect valve guides for wear; check valve stem-to-guide clearance; determine necessary action.	P-3			✓	362–364	118
10. Inspect valves and valve seats; determine necessary action.	P-3			✓	378–383	127, 128
11. Check valve spring assembled height and valve stem height; determine necessary action.	P-3			✓	384	129
12. Inspect valve lifters; determine necessary action.	P-2			✓	406–409	135

	Task	Priority	MLR	AST	MAST	Text Page #	Task Page #
13.	Inspect and/or measure camshaft for runout, journal wear, and lobe wear.	P-2			✓	410	138, 139
14.	Inspect camshaft bearing surface for wear, damage, out-of-round, and alignment; determine necessary action.	P-3			✓	410	140
C.	**Engine Block Assembly Diagnosis and Repair**						
1.	Remove, inspect, or replace crankshaft vibration damper (harmonic balancer).	P-2		✓	✓	335	165, 188
2.	Disassemble engine block; clean and prepare components for inspection and reassembly.	P-1			✓	332–336	108
3.	Inspect engine block for visible cracks, passage condition, core and gallery plug condition, and surface warpage; determine necessary action.	P-2			✓	346–347; 443–444	150
4.	Inspect and measure cylinder walls/sleeves for damage, wear, and ridges; determine necessary action.	P-2			✓	445	151
5.	Deglaze and clean cylinder walls.	P-2			✓	447–448	152
6.	Inspect and measure camshaft bearings for wear, damage, out-of-round, and alignment; determine necessary action.	P-3			✓	470–471	153
7.	Inspect crankshaft for straightness, journal damage, keyway damage, thrust flange and sealing surface condition, and visual surface cracks; check oil passage condition; measure end play and journal wear; check crankshaft position sensor reluctor ring (where applicable); determine necessary action.	P-1			✓	462–463	161, 162, 183
8.	Inspect main and connecting rod bearings for damage and wear; determine necessary action	P-2			✓	468–470	163, 173, 184
9.	Identify piston and bearing wear patterns that indicate connecting rod alignment and main bearing bore problems; determine necessary action.	P-3			✓	432–433	143, 164, 185
10.	Inspect and measure piston skirts and ring lands; determine necessary action.	P-2			✓	421–422	147
11.	Determine piston-to-bore clearance.	P-2			✓	434; 505–507	154, 174, 186
12.	Inspect, measure, and install piston rings.	P-2			✓	433–435	145, 146

	Task	Priority	MLR	AST	MAST	Text Page #	Task Page #
13.	Inspect auxiliary shaft(s) (balance, intermediate, idler, counterbalance, or silencer); inspect shaft(s) and support bearings for damage and wear; determine necessary action; reinstall and time.	P-2			✓	461–462	166, 187
14.	Assemble engine block.	P-1			✓	494–508	189, 190
D.	**Lubrication and Cooling Systems Diagnosis and Repair**						
1.	Perform cooling system pressure and dye tests to identify leaks; check coolant condition and level; inspect and test radiator, pressure cap, coolant recovery tank, and heater core; determine necessary action.	P-1	✓	✓	✓	171–172	32, 33
2.	Identify causes of engine overheating.	P-1		✓	✓	173	41
3.	Inspect, replace, and adjust drive belts, tensioners, and pulleys; check pulley and belt alignment.	P-1	✓	✓	✓	173–174; 527	34
4.	Inspect and test coolant; drain and recover coolant; flush and refill cooling system with recommended coolant; bleed air as required.	P-1	✓	✓	✓	174–175	37
5.	Inspect, remove, and replace water pumps.	P-2		✓	✓	168–169	38, 194
6.	Remove and replace radiator.	P-2		✓	✓	164;171	39, 195
7.	Remove, inspect, and replace thermostat and gasket/seal.	P-1	✓	✓	✓	162–163	36, 193
8.	Inspect and test fan(s) (electrical or mechanical), fan clutch, fan shroud, and air dams.	P-1		✓	✓	170	40, 196
9.	Perform oil pressure tests; determine necessary action.	P-1		✓	✓	305–306	103
10.	Perform engine oil and filter change.	P-1	✓	✓	✓	186–190	209
11.	Inspect auxiliary coolers; determine necessary action.	P-3		✓	✓	200–201	44
12.	Inspect, test, and replace oil temperature and pressure switches and sensors.	P-2		✓	✓	193	45
13.	Inspect oil pump gears or rotors, housing, pressure relief devices, and pump drive; perform necessary action.	P-2			✓	193–197	43, 191